Behold the Personal Maine Coon

By Phyllis Stiebens

D1710816

Œ

Strategic Book Publishing and Rights Co.

Strategic Book Publishing and Rights Co., LLC
USA | Singapore

For information about special discounts for bulk purchases, please contact Strategic Book Publishing and Rights Co. Special Sales, at bookorder@sbpra.net.

ISBN: 978-1-68181-912-9

Book Design: Suzanne Kelly

Acknowledgements

Thank you to Rianna for your editing help, you were such a blessing. Thank you to Sharon for helping me get the poly chapter in works, I needed that push. Thank you to my husband, John, for encouraging me when things were not so fun to work on again and again. Thank you to all the Maine Coon cats over the many years that have brought me so much pleasure and affection. Thank you to all the Maine Coon cat people who enjoyed sharing their beautiful photos, even when I asked for them more than twice. And, most of all, thank You, my Lord Jesus, for Your continued presence and blessing in my life! Without You I am nothing!

Table of Contents

Introduction

The Maine Coon cat is a valued breed of feline around the world. With its extra-large size, long silky coat, and family oriented personality, it is truly a one of a kind type of cat. Many folks call the cats their "puppy-kitties" for their endearing attachment traits. Get a Maine Coon cat, and you will see what all the excitement is about. But watch out . . . one may not be enough!

Kumskaka Bilagaana of Shedoros, "Billy."
Dorothea Scibura, Germany

CHAPTER 1
One Shaggy Beginning

Wackymoon Oreo PP, brown tabby female, 2012. Annelies Miller, Holland

Where in this world did this big, furry feline come from? How did such a gentle giant of a cat become an all-time favorite breed? What circumstances created such a large cat? Is this cat here to last? Questions like this are often asked to breeders of the Maine Coon cat. The answers can be simple and complicated at the same time.

The Maine Coon cat is an American breed. It originated in the Atlantic Northeast of the United States, specifically the state of Maine. A ship-building center and busy seaport, Maine hosted many visitors from all over our world. There are many romantic stories about how this breed of cat might have happened. The Vikings, Queen Marie Antoinette, being part raccoon (genetically impossible), and the shipping trade are all in the story books. Perhaps it is a combination of these stories. The domestic feline was not a native to North America until man brought her here. Seafaring cats were vital to ships in keeping the rat populations under control. Disease and filth were minimized with the help of the cat. Both seamen and visitors from all over the world sometimes traveled with their cats. When the ships made port in the new world, cats would jump ship and explore their new environments. Many of those cats made themselves comfortable, and then stayed behind. Thus starts the beginning of one such traveling feline breed.

Indigo of Coonquistador, red-silver cameo male, one year old. Anna Krylova, Russia

Maine is a state where winter can stay six months of the year and the lake waters are frozen for at least three months. It was a very hardy place to live and our cats' ancestors adjusted to this environment. The original Maine Coon cats were smaller than the show cats you see today, but still were big felines. They were solid and heavy, with a thick, shaggy coat that kept the cat warm and dry. The winters were long and sometimes frigid, so only the strongest survived, which kept these cats robust and hardy. Paws were big and tufted like snowshoes, and ears were tall, and alert to any sound. Many of the original cats of Maine were also polydactyl, and these extra-size paws helped keep their bodies atop the deep snows, which helped a lot in hunting. They also sported a long plume of a tail to wrap around themselves, as needed. They were a working breed and excelled at the job of rodent population-control manager very well. They became friends with the people who moved to the area, and the two groups co-existed, becoming family. The cats roamed freely, although many became house kitties. They did not have the kitty litter and litter boxes that we have now though, so it was just easier for the cats to live outside and take care of business in the great outdoors.

The original Maine Coon cats are a natural cat, meaning, they adapted to their environment and were not produced by specific breeding plans from man. Those who were built to endure the fierce winters survived. Having a strong instinct, large size, and immense genetic diversity, this cat developed a very easy going and contently happy personality. Over many generations, the Maine Coon cat was born. As in other pedigreed cat breeds though, man often gets involved, and then changes the looks and sizes. We must be careful about inbreeding, or the strong and healthy "natural" cat that we speak of here, will no longer exist.

Inbreeding in any animal, domestic or wild, is a problem over time. No matter the species, there must be outcrossing and unrelated lines being added. For the Maine Coon cat, only one association still has its stud books open. By bringing in new F1 cats (first generation to be added to the Maine Coon gene pool), we can keep this lovely breed of cat healthy and long-living. It is a lengthy process and can be very costly, but it is worth it for the few breeders who still work at adding new foundation. Health and longevity, as well as keeping the true breed's easy-going temperaments, are all threatened when too much inbreeding is pursued. Our natural Maine Coons were very outcrossed by nature and were happy and healthy cats. We must keep this as an important part of our breed's future, not just the breed's past.

Praylyne Joy of Dawn, brown mackerel tabby-white female, F2, 2012. Lies Beth Hansen, Holland

**Praylyne One Nation Under God, "Michele," F2, brown mackerel tabby-white female, one year.
Phyllis Stiebens, Georgia, USA**

I have talked with people from Maine, including my own relatives who lived in Maine, and read many stories from breeders in Maine about these cats. No one quite agrees on the name of this cat in its beginning. Perhaps it varied across regions, or perhaps everyone used all the names. Some say the farmers called their cats *Shags* due to the long, shaggy coats they sported. Some say they called their cats the *Coon cat* due to the raccoon-type tails, especially noticeable in the brown tabby coloring. Others say they called their cats the *Maine cat* simply because they were proud of the cats found only in their state of Maine. There were many competitions among people then, and they would brag about who had the best Shag, smartest Shag, and so forth. Many farmers proudly showed their Shag cats off at county fair competitions. To a native Mainer, it did not matter if you called your cat a *Shag,* a *Coon cat,* or a *Maine cat*, as they all referred to the same cat. What mattered was who was the biggest, hairiest, and best in competition.

In the 1860s, these cats were at a peak of their popularity. The top Shags were competing for the award of "Maine State Champion Coon Cat." The decline of the Maine Coon started in London, England, about 1871, with the first cat show. This is where new and unusual cats were shown for the first time. In 1883, the Grand Cat Show in Boston brought many of these new and unusual breeds to the United States. About four hundred felines were seen during the two weeks of this first cat show, including Persians, Manx, and Siamese.

In May 1895, when the most famous and largest of the early shows was held at Madison Square Garden in New York City, it is said that the show was won hands down, first place and best of show by a brown tabby female Maine Cat named Cosie. This must have been a spectacular show, numbering 176 animals in all, including two ocelots, two wildcats, and three civet cats. Included in this large show were many of the new and unusual breeds from all over the world, and it was this pretty little American female who won best in show.

As late as 1899, the Coon cat still won some awards at this yearly show, but the new breeds were catching on. As the cat shows continued to spread across the U.S. and Britain, the new breeds gained popularity. Upper-class people dominated the shows and were interested in the Persian and Angora breeds and, later, the Siamese. Owning these cats became very fashionable, and the Coon cat fell way behind. Who wanted a tough, rugged cat from the backwoods of Maine when all the winners at the shows were now the new, gorgeous, fancy felines? Breeders of the ritzy breeds were growing in number and kittens sold fast, as the Coon cat continued to decline in popularity. As the American cat clubs started up, Coon cats were registered, but not very many. With economic problems, wars, and other things, the Coon cat literally fell out of awareness from all but the people in the state of Maine.

Jumping ahead to 1953, Coon cat supporters formed the Central Maine Coon Cat Club. They organized Coon cat-only shows and started gaining a small but faithful group of admirers. The pedigree name chosen for the Shag of Maine was the Maine Coon Cat. In 1967, they wrote up a standard and, a year later, formed the Maine Coon Breeders and Fanciers Association (MCBFA). They were very important in getting the Coon cat back into the public eye and supporting breeders who were working hard with this breed. Breeders were encouraged to register the cats in their breeding program, and litter-register each litter. This gives us the beginning "foundation" of the breed. In 1976, CFA (Cat Fanciers Association) gave the Maine Coon cat championship status, and the real, hard work was to begin.

Behold the Anthem of Nations PP, F3, blue/white male 2010. John Monster, Holland

The original founding fathers of this breed had a very long and hard battle to get this breed noticed. Persians were the popular breed of cat, and many people were none too friendly to the Maine Coon breeders. Some of the Persian breeders did not feel this "barn" cat had any right in a show hall. The show world was hard on the breeders then. They spent their money and tried to educate the judges, other breeds people, and the public, while getting nothing for their trouble. Some of our founding breeders were so discouraged at shows they commented about leaving early or crying over rude remarks and the behavior of others.

Closer Walk of Praylyne, "Cari," torti/white female, F2, 2000. Phyllis Stiebens, Georgia, USA

This behavior continued even up to the late 1980s, though perhaps not to the severity of the earlier years. Things got better as the years wore on. Our foundation breeders put in the hard work to get us started, and it really has paid off. Those breeders kept at it despite it all, and we should be very grateful to them. Breeders began to attend club meetings and helped put up and take down shows. They convinced other Maine Coon breeders and pet owners to show more, and the breed caught on with a bang! When the visiting public started to take notice of this large and beautiful cat, so did the judges. Finals were harder to accomplish in CFA (and still can be), but more plentiful in the other show associations.

Mary Lou holding Tom in 1956.
Mary Hagen, Ohio, USA

Kylie holding Trinity in 2007.
Phyllis Stiebens, Georgia, USA

Maine Coons are now being shown in great numbers and winning very well all over the world. The colors that seem to win the most are the brown or silver tabbies, although we have seen many red tabby or even solid or bi-color winners. Thanks to the breeders at the beginning, this breed has not disappeared. They are no longer the farm cat; instead, they have become a great family member and show cat. Persians have ranked as the number one breed of cat at show, worldwide, for a long time. The Maine Coon cat, though, has moved up into the number two position worldwide, and some people say the number one position in America! Requiring less work and care than a Persian, many people began to choose the Maine Coon. The Persian may stay number one with the show person and judge simply due to the *hard work* involved. A well-groomed Persian, for instance, is truly an amazing work of art. But many people do not want the constant work that the Persian and Himalayan demand, and thus choose the big and beautiful Maine Coon cat. The future for this breed looks good. The size is impressive, the coat is easy and lovely, and the health is strong. The personality of this breed is very "personal" and plain ol' happy. Since they also have such a beautiful look, they are growing by leaps and bounds in popularity. Keep an eye on that gentle American-made giant!

Nordic Breed PP We All Need Jesus, "Bennet," blue mackerel tabby male, F3. Phyllis Stiebens, Georgia, USA

Kumskaka I'll Join the Rocks, "Joyan," F4, silver tabby female. Phyllis Stiebens, Georgia, USA

CHAPTER 2
A Personal Breed

Hercule des Coons de Lysane, brown tabby male. Noemie Estingoy, France

The Maine Coon cat is a true American and started in much the same way as the American people. A few cats came from here and a few cats came from there. They mixed with those from somewhere else. We ended up with a happy, true-blue American. It was a tough world back then to conquer. Only the strong survived in the human world *and* in the animal world. This breed worked for his dinner and became a family pet while doing so. The cats adjusted to all situations they encountered, and just seemed happy to be a part of the human world.

Maine Coons are personable and cheerful. Many people do not know this and are very surprised when they buy their first cat or kitten. These cats adore their human families and will often show a deep and personal affection toward them. This is a very easy cat to join your family, but they still need some basic socializing and training to become the popular family pet we all adore. Most cats can become a pet, but the Maine Coon is a companion. Your kitten will follow you around the house, making sure he is near you, whatever you are doing.

Klaudia with Kiara Queen Silverbastis, red tabby/white. Gosia Zeszutek, Poland

The breeder that you get your kitten from has a responsibility to get your baby started right in the world. There are many things you must look for to find a reputable and responsible breeder. This is actually your first job as a kitten buyer. Do not choose a kitten just from pretty photos! Put in the work to find the right breeder, or you could end up very unhappy.

A good breeder does not just put two pretty cats together and make a litter of pretty babies. A good breeder begins with the history/pedigree of the cats being bred. You can start by asking how much inbreeding is in the litter you want a baby from. Any breed—domestic or wild, feline, canine, and everything else—needs a genetic diversity to be healthy. Not only does inbreeding create unhealthy animals, but it also can affect the personality. Some breeders just breed what they like to what they like and ignore the "signs" that they have a problem. Breeding and birthing problems are one sign of inbreeding, and can be ignored by some. When the cats they raise start to get aggressive and unfriendly, this starts the ruining of the breed. Who wants to buy a sassy and grouchy animal? Inbreeding is very easy to begin doing and

10

thus starts the end of a healthy breed. Show wins are one reason inbreeding can start. What do the judges like? If the cat being shown does not win, then some breeders will buy a different look to breed with. If they do not investigate extended pedigrees, they can be in trouble.

Oticami Picasso, black smoke male. Izabella and Robert Sitjka, China

Another reason inbreeding can start in a breed is to make one characteristic of the cat more extreme. Any trait can be exploited by consistent inbreeding. Here are a few of the most common reasons for inbreeding in Maine Coon cats:

- larger than normal adult size
- longer than normal length of muzzle
- taller than normal ears or taller than normal ear tufts
- longer than normal body, and
- more extreme, feral-facial expression.

Whether for personal likes, to increase sales of kittens, or to win more at shows (or a combination of all three), these changes in the breed can be very unhealthy. If inbreeding is done slightly, still using some out-cross lines, then setting a look is perfectly okay. But if done over decades, then the results are dangerous for the future of the breed. As a pet person, it is not your job to look at inbred or outcross pedigrees. It is your job to find a breeder who has healthy, happy, and robust Maine Coons. A Maine Coon is a family cat known for its size and personality, and we must treasure this or find another breed.

Phyllis Stiebens

Emil with Shedoros litter. Dorothea Scibura, Germany

Hannibal Silverbastis, silver tabby male. Gosia Zeszutek, Poland

Annelie with MaCoo's Business Class. Cindy deKoning, Holland

When we used to show back in the late 1980s, many of the Maine Coons in the show hall were so unfriendly that the judges called them the "mean coons." It took many years, and some breeders finally quitting, before things turned around. There are always some cats (of any breed) who do not like the show hall, however. If you attend a show and see some cats acting up, do not automatically assume they are inbred and the breeder is not doing a good job. Some cats just cannot handle the stress and noise of a show hall and need to be retired to a happy family life instead. If you see a cat you really like at a show, try to make arrangements to visit the home of this breeder and see how the cats behave in their own environment. You need to see how these cats are with their owners, their cat family, as well as how they react to visitors. Can you sit and talk to them and have a few come right over to visit? It is normal for many of the cats to watch you from a distance as they get to know you, but it should not be for very long. These cats are curious and will want to venture over and sniff and then start rubbing on you. Watch them to start playing with your shoe laces and rubbing their bodies along your arms and legs. If you are accepted as family within a reasonable amount of time, then this is a cattery where the lines will do well for your own family. Get involved and participate with each cat. Choosing a breeder means choosing that breeder's cattery.

How do you know a good breeder? Here is a simple list that you should go through while choosing a breeder to work with. Remember: the baby you are adopting was the breeder's baby first. You will need a working relationship so you can always get support from the breeder when you need it. Invest in a friendship of sorts so you can share updates and photos over the years.

Penshewa Farm Mister Murphy, Queenstars Cara Mia, Queenstars Farah Diba, and Queenstars Keiyla.
Pia Thurig-Ramseyer, Switzerland

Twelve things you want to consider in a breeder include:

A good breeder shows their cats in at least one association or has shown in the past. This is important since it will help you know that this breeder knows the correct standard for the breed and has learned proper care and grooming for the breed.

A good breeder does health testing. More about health issues will be mentioned later in this book, but if a breeder does no testing, you will have no idea what troubles could be ahead. Testing cannot guarantee 100 percent healthy cats. Even cats from tested lines can develop health problems. But get as much testing behind your baby as you can for your own sense of security.

A good breeder shows the facility of the cattery on the website. If you cannot go to the breeder's home in person to get your kitten, don't be afraid to ask for more photos of the cats in their environment. Do not buy where many cages, especially small ones, are seen. A cage may be needed in a sick room, or a birthing room. A walk-in pen may be used to keep boys separated from girls, but anyone who has walls lined with cages is not a good place to buy from. If you are able to visit the cattery, look for relaxed and happy Maine Coons who adore their people. Some Maine Coons are wary of strangers but should not be frightened of them. Sometimes a shy adult will avoid visitors. But just be sure the whole cattery group is not like this. Allow the cats to watch you and sniff you while you attempt a pet and then some neck scratching. Once they allow this and are purring, you are accepted, and you can then see the personalities of the cats at this cattery. Some Maine Coons are not wary of strangers and will grab you as soon as you walk in the door. It is not normal for an entire group to ignore visitors. It's an individual thing, and you should be able to make friends with a few within minutes.

Rainbow Cat Jolie of Merveillecoon, brown tabby-white female. Beata Zanati, Hungary

A good cattery is not overcrowded. If you visit in person, ask to see other rooms where cats also may be living. On occasion a breeder may have two or three litters close to one another and be very full with babies, but this should not be the norm. Six adult females and a couple of males, along with kittens and a few adolescents, is plenty to fill a cattery. Use your own judgment. There is no "rule" here.

A good cattery will be clean. You may always find loose litter on the floor and a dirty bowl in a sink, but you can tell a clean area. If you smell urine, it is possible they have a spraying male and this smell will not go away for some time. But take a look around and make sure that the cats are happy and healthy looking. Be alert for dripping eyes, sneezing, skin problems, or other signs of sickness (unless in a separated sick room).

A good breeder is transparent about potential problems or weaknesses in certain lines. There is no disease-free line or genetic problem-free cattery. If you are being told such things, do not work with this breeder. There are always problems of some sort, and if you are told of a problem in a line or litter, do not be afraid. This is a breeder who is being honest with you, and that is an important beginning. If a breeder is new or being mentored, they may not know the lines well, and we suggest you then contact those who are mentoring them.

Kaleb with Behold King Faergus, black male, ten weeks old. Katrina Nager, Florida, USA

A good breeder has a healthy diet for the cats they own and raise. Setting out kibbles and nothing else is not a proper or healthy-enough diet for most cats. There are many types of dry food now and some are healthy while others are not. Since the cat is a carnivore, many breeders feed a raw meat program, which is very healthy. But not all breeders can or want to feed raw. Diet will be discussed in a later chapter, and what you want to feed is your choice. You will be able to tell a lot from observing the cats in person. Are their eyes bright and are the cats alert and happy? Do they have healthy fur and skin?

A good breeder should take some time to get to know you before approving you for the purchase of one of its babies. Some will ask for details of your home. Others may just ask what you want in a pet. Make sure you are buying from a breeder who cares about the future of the Maine Coon breed as well as the kittens they are selling. If you are not a breeder, do not even attempt to ask for breeding rights on a kitten. All responsible breeders will either sell their kittens with a neuter/spay agreement or have them neutered or spayed before leaving their home. To become a Maine Coon breeder takes many years of research, learning, and showing in premiership (neutered championship class). If purchasing from a newer breeder, ask some questions. A newer breeder should be under the "mentorship" of a long-term breeder.

A good breeder should have a pet contract that requires a basic set of rules for you to follow. You may not always like the rules in the contract, but they are important for the cat and his future. The basics every breeder should have you agree to include never letting you declaw the cat or allowing the cat loose outdoors. The contract should require you to neuter/spay by a certain age (usually by 7 months) and to provide a nutritious diet and veterinary care for the life of your cat.

A good breeder will not allow the kittens to leave their home before the age of twelve weeks (and sometimes much later). They will provide registration papers, although some will not give those until you have the kitten neutered or spayed.

Kaleb with Behold King Faergus, black male, eighteen months old. Katrina Nager, Florida, USA

Behold Duke Kahanamoku Ali'l, silver tabby male, two years old. Lisa Pakosh, Bahamas

A good breeder does not continually sell "cheap deals." To provide good quality care, constant deals are not possible to give. Sometimes a breeder will have lower-priced kittens due to lesser quality/size, an older age kitten, or a spayed/neutered adult. These are fine for one-time deals. Just remember that a rule of thumb is "you get what you pay for."

Gabriel with Cancion de Cunalorele, cream tabby male. Monica Sanchez, Brazil

A good breeder has a good reputation. Ask other breeders, as well as pet buyers, what they know about the breeder you have in mind. Their experiences can help you decide whether you want to buy a kitten from someone. Do not be fooled by backyard breeders. Kitten mills can have very appealing websites with great pictures. They often use titles of ancestral cats and health testing results of other catteries to look reputable. Most of these backyard breeders have never lifted a finger to earn any titles, let alone test any of their own breeding stock. So make sure you ask lots of questions before committing to a purchase. A newer breeder may not yet know the answers to your questions, and that is part of his learning, so do not be afraid of this breeder, unless he is not being mentored. If you want a kitten from a new breeder, just ask to talk to her mentor.

Growing a personal Maine Coon starts with the breeder and continues with you. Breeding is not easy. Breeding is meant only for people who have a complete devotion and knowledge of the Maine Coon. Good breeders will engage their children, grandchildren, nieces, nephews, and all other family members to handle and socialize the kittens right from the beginning. It makes a difference when kittens have access to people who love them.

Socializing begins with the breeder. When you get your kitten at around three months of age, he is only starting to learn what is required of him. This is a very slow maturing breed, so even though your cat looks big to you, he is really like your little toddler. He must be loved with affection and discipline. You must continue the socializing and training that the breeder began for you. All cats require pretty much the same thing to become a valued member of your family, but this large breed responds well to a little special handling.

Like little children, your Maine coon may not always be willing to do what you want him to do, and when you want him to do it. The rule of thumb with this breed is that you are the boss, not the cat. If you want the cat to be groomed, it's time for grooming. If you say no to a dinner table "attack," then you must be firm in your actions. You need never be angry with the kittens, as they just need to be taught you are the "mama." Mother cats are lenient to a point, and then can become quite rough with some smacks and bites to get their kittens to listen. If you have ever seen this, you may think the Mom cat is being really mean, but she is not. She disciplines in her own way, and then goes back to licking and loving on them. They know Mom cares, and they learn when Mom has had enough. The kittens do not always listen, as they are babies and learn as they grow. Remember this in your own training times. If you become angry, the cat will avoid that training, and it will be much harder to train the cat to cooperate. Handle with firmness, but love.

Maine Coons grow up as easy-going in all they do. They are kitten-like, even as adults, and are relaxed about life. Since they are so in love with their family members, they will respond to training with ease. Your cat will have fun just spending time with you, whether for training or affection. Once you are her family, she never wants to be parted from you!

Kittens are active and curious and can be a real handful for some families. The babies do not just sit around and purr (although they do this a lot). Like any toddler, they often can get themselves into trouble. Imagine the baby who will jump where you may not want him to, possibly knocking things off when he gets there. With age, the cats become more graceful, jumping easily and smoothly to their favorite nap spot. The heavier a male gets (and some females), the clumsier he may become though. He knows he can jump to a spot, but he does not think about the weight force that will hit the spot when he gets there. Maine Coons are sometimes comical to watch. They take everything in stride and never seem to mind our laughter—it does appear at times that they are clowns just for our benefit. As your Maine Coon grows and matures, he will still make mistakes. But he will also amuse you, even while breaking a rule or two.

For the cat owner, your number one job in raising a happy gentle giant is to love on them. Like our human children, cats all have individual personalities. There are many breed traits that are pretty standard for all Maine Coons, but some cats have a unique thing they love or hate. As the "parent," it is your job to know these things and act accordingly. The breed characteristics (in Chapter 3) will help you see some areas to train for and against, but you must learn your own kitten. No matter what you train for, do it all with affection so your kitten will bloom. Socializing is your next job and a very important part of his development. When you are growing a gentle giant, you do not want a cat that freaks out over something silly (if ever). Things they are not used to can be frightening and can cause stress and fear to a cat. Get them used to everything you can. And think about what you want the adult to do or not to do. Start the training while in kitten hood and keep at it. What they see as being the norm of life will never frighten them. You are about to become a Maine Coon parent. Are you ready?

Big Kitty Oxana, black female, eleven months old. Magdalena Karlsson, Sweden

CHAPTER 3

Characteristics of the Maine Coon Cat

Paco Rabanne, brown tabby male, two years old. Audra Navikiene, Lithuania

The Maine Coon is a semi-longhair cat. Although the coat quality fluctuates with breeding times, season, and neuter/spay status, it is never a shorthair cat. The outer coat is of a soft and silky texture, flowing softly against the body contours. The under coat is more shaggy and of a fuzzier texture and requires more grooming to prevent matting. Weekly grooming is the rule, but more is required in the spring and fall, or during show season. If you live in a colder climate, your cat may grow a thicker winter coat. In spring, you would then have more undercoat to comb out so as to prevent tangles and mats.

Yowie's Power, black smoke-white, six months old. Simone Soderberg, Denmark

The tail is long, about the length of the body, with a thick plume of beautiful fur. I am sure our original native cats used their tails as thick blankets in the bitter cold of the American Northeastern winters. Body and facial characteristics are often not as important to the pet owner as it is to the breeder or show person. Your pet is your baby and, if not being shown, it does not matter how closely the cat fits the show standard of any of the show registries. The official CFA breed standard is listed in Chapter 12 and can be seen in full on their website. As an example though, here is a simplified description of the physical characteristics:

The body is rectangular. The legs are tall and the body is long, with a tail that should be as long as the body is from shoulder to hips. The tail is covered in long fur. Body fur is shorter on the shoulders and face, then gets longer and shaggier under the belly, britches, and ruff. Maine Coon babies typically do not start to grow that lovely coat and tail until about 8 months of age. Kittens have a baby coat and can go through a gangly stage, where parts are not so uniform in contrast to other parts of their bodies. The older the Maine Coon, the more all his parts blend and look proper. The face is a beautiful flow of features, including round eyes with just a pinch at the outer corners; a wide, thick muzzle and chin that line up and a profile that has a soft bend at the upper area of the nose. Ears are wide at bottom, placed about an ear's width apart, and preferably with ear tufts on top. Long hairs grow in the ears, curling around behind the ear. Many cats grow long, frizzy ear curls behind the ears that can sometimes mat if not combed. They are adorable when sticking out on the sides of the head.

Have you ever seen a fully-coated Maine Coon photo that you admire greatly, and compare to another photo with a shorter coat and wondered why this is? Once you know the breed's characteristics and their growth pattern, this will be easy for you to determine details of the cat in the photo. As kittens, babies have very little coat. They may be fluffy and soft while others may be shorter coated, depending on the season. Typically though, kittens do not get much adult coat and fluff before seven months of age. At this age of development, the tail starts to fluff out and the neck ruff starts to fill in. These will continue to grow and fill out if the kitten is neutered/spayed about the same time. Hormones can have a devastating effect on a cat coat! Once hormones move in, the cat eats less and loses condition. There are some hormone therapies that some breeders use to help keep coat on a breeding age adult, for showing and photography. Typically though, if you see a Maine Coon in a thin coat, just assume the cat has active hormones. If you are a pet person who is not going to be breeding, then do not delay the neuter/spay appointment for your baby. By one year of age, and no hormones to get in the way, you will have a very beautiful thick coated and stunning Maine Coon baby!

Tw'Ice, odd eye white. Nynke van Holten, Holland

Phyllis Stiebens

Furlongcoons Redman, red tabby-white, three years old. Marianne Verschueren, Belgium

Oticami Herman, 14-week-old male, silver mackerel tabby-white. Izabella and Robert Sijka, China

**Allegiance Love Legeng of Toruk Makto PP, one year old, brown mackerel tabby.
Elena Udovenko, Bulgaria**

This is a larger than normal size cat. Maine coons have an admirable height and length. Add in the solid boning and thick, bushy coat, and you have one large feline. The males are bigger than females, and grow the wider tomcat heads, making them beautiful cats to admire. Males that are neutered are easily twenty pounds on average and some getting many more pounds than this. Females tend toward a spayed weight of about thirteen pounds but, obviously, can be more pounds also. When in a healthy, fit body, thirteen to twenty-plus pounds is a good weight for this cat to carry. The rumors of cats weighing thirty pounds and up are just rumors, however. When confronted with a scale, people who brag at having such large cats are quite embarrassed to find their cats closer to twenty pounds in actual weight. Yes, these cats look huge. With a thick coat, it is easy to exaggerate the weight.

Maine Coon cats are a naturally hardy creation. The breed has not been played with by man, as many weaker breeds have. Some breeds cannot even deliver a litter of kittens without emergency vet visits and C-sections. Some cannot breathe well, and others cannot jump or climb. Look at the pushed-in-face of the Persian, Himalayan, and Exotic Shorthair; the spinal problems of the Manx and Cymric; the skin problems of the Sphynx; and the frail, tiny frame of the exotic Siamese. You will not see any of this on a Maine Coon. They have a strong past and a strong future, as long as man does not interfere with nature's "mountain man."

This is a quiet cat. Maine Coons have a very soft voice in general, especially compared to the size of the body. A chirp of sorts is their call and conversation tone. A happy Maine Coon will chatter with you and tell you what he thinks he needs. You will find one, on occasion, with a louder voice. We laugh at this. It is not the norm though, and even those who do talk a bit louder are still quieter than cats from noisy breeds.

Merete with Gentle Powers Felizia. Nina Nilsen, Norway

Maine Coons take a long time to grow and mature. This is one of the reasons why your breeder would not let you take your kitten home when he was a tiny and extra cute little character. Kittens are not generally weaned before seven weeks of age. In the following month or more, that kitten must learn to eat on his own, use a litter box faithfully, love his humans in the nicest ways, and start his scratching-post training. This is in addition to starting vaccinations and vet care. Twelve weeks is the absolute earliest that any reputable breeder will let you get your kitten. Some may make you wait until the cat is four to five months of age. Do not be upset over this. Your kitten will not be physically mature until well into his fourth year. You will have plenty of months with an energetic kitten and all those fun antics as he grows to full maturity.

As a kitten grows and slowly matures, he will change in looks, not just in size and weight. If you choose a kitten as a little baby, you will be really surprised when you receive new photos from your breeder every two to three weeks. This is one extra reason some breeders hold their kittens past the twelve-week mark: For a person who wants to *show*, you cannot tell the show-quality of a kitten before about five months. Breeders get better at this when they know their own lines, but it is still a gamble. Once the kittens are sixteen weeks or so, then it starts to get easier to see who is blooming better than the others. The show halls are full of good Maine Coons, so to have a chance at wins, you will need better than good. Enjoy watching an energetic kitten grow and change and get ready for the day when he can come home with you.

Perhaps adopting a young adult is better for your family. You get to skip the crazy baby days. A young adult has already started its scratching-post training and *no-no* list, is fully vaccinated, and has been neutered or spayed. Kittens require more work, and young adults can be better for those who do not have the time and patience to devote to the early training and care. Young adults may take a little longer to adjust to a new home and family, but they all do adjust. Remember, a Maine Coon is not fully mature in mind, body, or size until approximately four years of age. Some people prefer taking on an adult cat, who is still a very playful cat with his own unique personality, but has outgrown some of that first training stage of young kittens. Considering how long they live, you will still have a good long time with your Maine Coon family member.

The Maine Coon cat has many fun and unique traits. Once you have a Maine Coon in your family, you will see many of these traits in your own baby. As an individual, you may see many more fun things that are unique to your kitten. Head-butting is a common trait, which they simply love to do. When a huge and heavy male head-butts you (and you don't see it coming), it will get your attention quickly. They do it out of great affection, so lean down to talk to them face to face and watch for them to bump heads with you. Rubbing their whole body on you, as they do to another cat, is something else they often do. This rubbing ensures that you wear the cat's scent and he wears yours. This is your cat's way of telling everyone that you belong together. If you ignore their first attempts for attention, they will proceed more strongly. Some cats will wrap themselves around your calves or plop in front of your feet as you are trying to walk around them. Other cats will kiss, lick, and wrap themselves around your neck. Many will groom their owners on the hand, the foot, the leg or the head, whatever it takes to get your attention. Watch for the *dopey* look of love in their eyes. This love-sick expression is just for you, the *mama*. While they are friendly and happy with all people, this special look is only for his special family.

Behold blue male kitten at ten weeks called Peeta Mellark. Phyllis Stiebens, Georgia, USA

LaMirage by Imagine Glamour, red silver-white, three years old. Radka Vacikova, Czech Republic

Just Vanilla of Mainly Queens, white, one year old. Nynke van Holten, Holland

One rather fun (or not-so-fun) trait is what we call the *crazed moments*. The kitten gets it in his mind to run full speed and, if on slippery floors (like linoleum), he will be fun to watch. He may run in place for some seconds, like a cartoon character, and then burst into full speed, only to collide into a wall or piece of furniture. Then the whole procedure starts back up for the next wall. If you have more than one Maine Coon, it can be a very noisy game when they are all playing the crazy game at once. Thank goodness the game does not last long and they go back to relaxing. Some people describe the game humorously as "sounding like a herd of elephants."

Each Maine Coon will have his favorite place to relax with his human family. Some just like to lie on his human's lap, some the neck, and some beside you. They may not just lay and purr quietly like you may think. There are many who are just too happy to sit quietly and relax. Some will rub on you repeatedly, until you are laughing with glee. Whatever you are working on with your hands may become where your Maine Coon baby will want to be. When you work at your computer, you may find your kitten lying on the keyboard. Some cats will hang over the screen and there are some who will lay on your lap while you work. When you read a book, you may find your baby getting into your line of eyesight. This can be annoying (especially if trying to study for a test), but it is just his way of getting attention. Your kitten is like a small child. You will find that, if you spend some special time with him first, he will then lie quietly near you or play until he falls asleep.

Vennoa's King Lui, red tabby/white, one year old. Annett Strietzel, Germany

Nascat Gwydion of Gradach, brown tabby-white, ten years old. Donna Hinton, Texas, USA

When it comes time to nap, some kittens will want to be on your lap. Others will want to be at your feet or beside you. Still others want to sleep wrapped around your neck. For those requiring a neck wrap, it may be fun while he is a kitten, but wait until you have twenty pounds of muscle and fur trying to snuggle into your hair.

Expect your kitten to offer his help while you are doing your household chores. Although you may not think you need your Maine Coon's help, it really can make a boring job a little more pleasurable. Try folding a batch of laundry with your kitty in the laundry basket. Try sweeping or mopping the floor with a bundle of fur in the way. Some may run when a vacuum is turned on and others will lie in its way, watching it come to them as if a game. Try cleaning out a dishwasher or refrigerator with their assistance. They surely have their own way of doing things and can really be clowns.

The favorite game of many Maine Coons is played from the top of their scratching post (or dresser). They love to be up high and look down on their world. What joy the cats get from waiting for a human to venture past! Patting the human head with a paw brings such ornery looks to their faces that you cannot be upset with them. It's a game *they* win every time.

One common trait of this breed is stirring water. When we got our first Maine Coons, it drove us crazy for a while, but we learned to live with it. Now we try to warn others of this fun trait. This breed of cat loves to stir the water before they take a drink. Do not buy a small water bowl or you will be cleaning up a mess every day. We recommend putting a large dog-size, heavy-ceramic crock on the floor with a towel or rug under it. Or consider keeping the bowl in a sink. These cats have so much fun playing in the water! It can be very entertaining to watch while they get the water circulating and then lean down to drink with the water moving. Once the water is moving, some will drink from the bowl and others will scoop up water in their paws for a drink. Then they will go back for another stir and scoop. There are some cats who prefer the trickling faucet. Those will scoop a sip, often getting head and ears in the water and some even put their mouths into the water and drink as it pours. It can be messy, but is a refreshing game for them. The fun does not fully stop until the water faucet is turned off. Some Maine Coons love to play in the bath or shower water also. This can be more fun when there is a child already in the tub so that the game is ongoing. If you add bubble bath, that makes it even more fun for child and cat alike. For a fun and *clean* game, just fill a bowl or bucket with water and stand back. To make it a little more exciting, float a toy in it and grab the camera. The fun will last a long time. Keep a towel handy if you are indoors for this wet game.

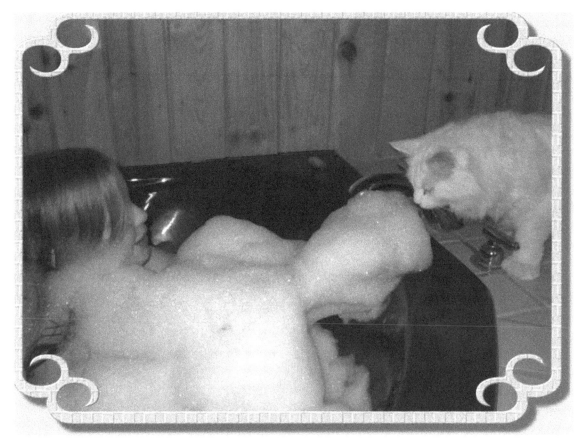

Kylie, with Princess Bubbles, white female, one year old. Katrina Nager, Florida, USA

Novuelle Nascensy, white, three months old. Alena Mosna, Slovakia

Quindra's China Rose, two years old, silver torbie. Janneke Vande Zand, Holland

Amy with Frozen Moon's Double Espresso. Carolien Ossewaarde, Holland

Like all breeds of cats, the Maine Coon loves to play. Each cat has his own favorite toys and you will learn over time which ones your baby loves most. A favorite for most is the feather-stick toy. It is also a favorite tool for many breeders who use it to get the cat's attention so that photographs can be taken with the cat looking in the right direction. Some Maine Coons become very loud with growls if they get the tassels or feathers into their mouths. They see this as a bird and it's their catch. Trying to pull toys out of the cat's mouth, to get back to the fun, is a lot of work, and some feather toys do not survive. When not being used, keep the toys put away where the cats cannot find them. Watch out especially for the tassel ones, since some cats will try to eat those tassels, which would be very dangerous for them. Be warned that some cats learn to open cupboards, so keep this in mind when trying to find a safe place to hide toys.

Mellocats Guinness PP, brown tabby, eighteen months. Sandra Tassinari, Massachusetts, USA

33

CHAPTER 4
Choices to Make

Two litters of ten-week-old kittens at Patayan cattery. Solenn Helias, Serbia

Once you have found your breeder, you can enjoy finding your kitten. Do you want a typical color or pattern, like the brown, red, or silver tabby? Or perhaps you want a colorful calico, or regal solid black. Some people like to find a uniquely marked or colored kitten, a "one-of-a-kind" type. Maine Coons come in all colors and patterns except color point (like a Siamese), so you can have a lot of fun looking for that one who steals your heart.

Here are photos of a few very uniquely marked Maine Coons that may really catch your eye.

Los Miticos Sweet Fairytale, blue torti-white, three months old. Sabina Ostermann, Spain

Siduroy Jasmine, torti-white. thirteen weeks old. Miriam Muller, Holland

Wild Eddy of Secret Schatz, blue-white. Esther Guggenbuhl, Switzerland

"Sweet expression female," Kumskaka Has No Other Choice PP, "Gilli," silver torbie, three years old.
Phyllis Stiebens, Georgia, USA

There are a variety of *looks* to the Maine Coon breed. Each breeder brings his own individuality when interpreting the Maine Coon standards. Some people prefer a feral expression, which gives the impression of toughness or of a wild cat. Some people like a baby face and big, imploring eyes. Ears, too, can have a little variety—there is the old-fashioned look with smaller ears and the more modern look of much larger ears. Ears come with or without the lovely curls and ear tips, which you may like or dislike.

"Feral expression female," American Beautys Ola, brown torbie, five years old.
Petra Oosterbroek, Holland

Then there is the eye color to consider. The normal eye color is gold, though some cats have green. You can find blue eyes or odd eyes in a solid white Maine Coon. Sometimes a colored cat has uniquely colored eyes, which is extremely handsome and not real common. If you find one and it is for sale, you might want to buy this one quickly.

GOLD eye female, Behold Windows-of-Heaven Open PP, shell cameo, eight months old. Phyllis Stiebens, Georgia, USA

GREEN eye female, Iris by Imagine Glamour, blue tabby/white two years old, Radka Vacikova, Czech Republic

Odd-eye white, Diamantcriss Luxerycoons, five months old. Alena Mosna, Slovakia

Some people are more interested in the whole package than in the small details. Whether or not you care about the details, enjoy looking and thinking about what you would like in your Maine Coon baby. A breeder has a little bit of fun mixing different looks and details to make his own special look, and although nobody else may agree with him, we all have that perfect cat in our mind. Your job now is to go in search of your perfect one that you dream of.

Now there is color to consider. Do you want a solid colored Maine Coon with the color solid to the root? Your cat can come in solid black or solid blue. There is also a solid red or solid cream, but that is for breeder information only. These cats look like a tabby, so for the pet person, we will not attempt to show solid reds or creams here. One of my own favorite colors is created by adding smoking to a solid color! I love how an effect called smoke alters a solid color. Smoke is caused by a gene that inhibits the color on the fur close to the skin of the cat, making the fur whitish near the body and darker at the tips. On a solid black, blue, bicolor, or tri-color, the smoking effects are breathtaking. We will not show all the variety in solid smoke colors here, but you can find them on many websites and on Maine Coon cat sites.

Notice how the silver gene can change a lovely color into something breathtaking.

Black, Rotcat Lilith. Sera Lehtonen, Finland

Black smoke, Macawimosi Ryusei's Nahuel. Carolien Ossewaarde, Holland

Blue, Hades du Val d'Azzarine. Christele Benoit, France

Blue smoke/white, CoonCatCabin Shine Keeko Shine. Danielle Carroll, Georgia, USA

If you add red or cream to these dark, solid colors, you get flashy females. Tortoiseshell (called torti for short) and blue-cream are normally female-only colors, but on a rare occasion a male can be found.

Tortoiseshells, Volcano Yojoa, Velor Alsuhail, and Venture Joyful, all of Greengrove, four months old. Marcin Skwarczynski, Poland

Smoke Torti, Dinkidi Polly Flinders. Cynthia Harper, Australia

Blue cream (also called blue torti), Dinkidi Breakin Dawn, "Betty." Cynthia Harper, Australia

Blue cream smoke/white (also called smoked dilute torti), Zaika Family Star.
Danielle Carroll, Georgia, USA

Do you love the tabbies? There are a huge variety of these colors and they come in two main patterns: classic-blotched and mackerel. Some cat associations also allow a ticked tabby and a spotted tabby, but no information will be given on those colors here. They are lovely and more about them can be seen on breeders' websites.

Tabbies come in a "with white" variety and a "without white" variety. Some of the tabby colors for females can also be multi-colored (like the tri-colors mentioned above), and these are called torbies or patched tabbies.

Here are the most common colors for Maine Coon cats and the most popular worldwide.

Red Mackerel tabby/white, Oticami Impact. Izabella and Robert Sijka, China

Red smoke (in the tabby version, it is called cameo or red-silver tabby), Aglowcoons Western Rose. Beata Smith, Hungary

Phyllis Stiebens

Cream tabby, White Rocke Caruso. Oxana Abdulkhakova, Russia

Cream smoke (in the tabby version, it is called a cream cameo or cream-silver tabby), Grandeur Tikvah. Heather Barnetson, Ontario, Canada

44

Brown tabby, Cattycats Magical Obsedian. Carolien Ossewaarde, Holland

**Brown torbie (also called brown patched tabby), Bearcloud Honeymoon Croon.
Carolien Ossewaarde, Holland**

Silver tabby, Rivendell. Esther Klock, Holland

Silver torbie/white (also called Silver patched tabby), Aglowcoons Vicky Barcelona. Beata Smith, Hungary

Blue tabby, Prairiebaby Polly of Oticami. Izabella and Robert Sijka, China

Blue-silver tabby/white, Ducky of Talina City. Natalya Andreyuk, Russia

Phyllis Stiebens

Blue mackerel torbie (also called blue mackerel patched tabby), Oticami Cassie Blue. Izabella and Robert Sijka, China

Blue-silver torbie (also called blue-silver patched tabby), Marvelcoon Madlene. Natalya Andreyuk, Russia

Sometimes the silver gene will give a more smoking white undercoat on a cat. The results are a very white looking tabby, and a highly desired coloring occurs. A silver tabby or a cameo tabby can both become a shaded or a shell. Shaded means about three-quarters of the hair shaft is white, and shell means about nine-tenths of the hair shaft is white. Both are very beautiful!

Shaded silver torbie, Nektarcats Like a Lily. Phyllis Stiebens, Georgia, USA

Shaded cameo, Joy de Riviera Coon. Valerie Ansaldi, Italy

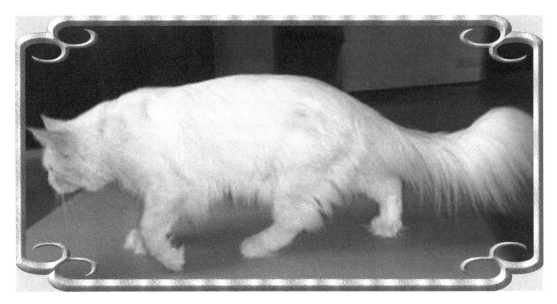

Shell cameo, Behold Windows-of-Heaven Open PP. Phyllis Stiebens, Georgia, USA

Another favorite is a lovely solid white, which can be extremely elegant. There are no markings, shading, smoking, or effects on a solid white. This is a very sparkly color on a big Maine Coon cat. Sometimes a white is born with a tiny colored spot on top of its head. If small enough, it will go away with age. This sparkly color is a peek into what color they are genetically masking. Many times a breeder has to breed their solid white to find out what color they are masking (you get the idea once colored babies are born in a litter).

White, Kumskaka Bilagaana of Shedoros. Dorothea Scibura, Germany

Maine Coons can be without white or with white in all colors. The white can be added to a color in varying degrees. White can start with just the toes and a bib under the cat's chin. A cat with a touch of white on paws and bib, will look like he's wearing a tuxedo. These would be called a *bicolor* for solids and *with white* for a tabby.

When the whole front of the cat is white and there are only spots of color on the back, head, and tail, then you have a Harlequin. The last step between Harlequin and solid white is a Van, where the cat just has color on the head and the tail.

Van smoke torti, Sleepy Hollow Queen Viktoria, two years old. Radka Vacikova, Czech Republic

Harlequin black/white, Zuberi Dejon von Thivoedone, one year old. Netty Schipper, Holland

Then there are the tri-colors to look into, which are the same as just mentioned above with the white, except adding a second color. Your black bi-color becomes a calico and your blue bi-color becomes a dilute calico. Again, these are normally female-only colors. And adding the silver gene can make them even more beautiful!

Calico, Kagatka Baccaracoon. Ewa Szczucka, Poland

Dilute calico, RP Cathouse Baby Blue Born. Stella Diane, Maryland, USA

Harlequins Oticami Kassu, blue-silver tabby/white male; Oticami Kivi, silver torbie/white female; and Oticami Kiara, silver torbie female. Izabella and Robert Sijka, China

Some people choose their kitten on a total look and others choose a specific color. Your heart will tell you when you have seen or met one that gives you those goose-bumps. If you have found a breeder to work with and have a good idea of what color you want, the next question is about gender.

Do you want a male or a female? Are there any differences? This breed is a special affectionate breed and either gender is good for a pet. There are some basic differences in them, however, but each cat is an individual and can just be themselves and not fit into any group mentioned.

Boys, in general, have a more laid-back temperament. We breeders, with love, call our boys the big-dummies. This is no way impugning to them, it just describes a difference in the boy verses the girl, so we use it here. Boys do not seem to mind changes to their lives as much, and are easier going as far as visitors to their home. They are bigger in size and weight than a girl, even a large girl. And one part that separates them from the girls is their male heads. These heads widen with age. They have fatter cheek-bones, wider ear-set, and a general masculine appearance. Being large and heavy, they tend to be a little more awkward in their games, which can make them the family clown to enjoy for years.

Girls, in general, are very smart. Where the boys seem too *dumb* to figure things out, and thus get into less trouble, the girls typically get into everything at least once. Perhaps the boys are smart enough not to get into trouble, whereas the females cannot control themselves—who is the smart one here? But in general the girls have to check everything out. They seem to have to know how to get in where you do not want them to be. Girls are more agile, and so can get up into areas you would think no cat of this size could get to. Girls tend to attach themselves strongly to their family with a deep love. Although boys do this also, it seems at times that the boys can adjust to new people and homes a little easier than the females tend to. Females tend to dislike changes to their home and routine a bit more than the males do.

Both the male and female bond deeply with their family, and can adjust to a new home with ease, if given a little time. The younger a Maine Coon, the faster they adjust to a new home and family. With food they love and affection from family, this breed of cat can move right into a new home with ease. Adopt one of any age and enjoy them as your adopted children! Now go find that dream baby of yours, but watch out . . . sometimes one is not enough. A pair of Maine Coons is truly double the fun.

Adult male look: Dynamicats KidRock, brown tabby/white male. Marja Brouwer, Holland

Adult female look: MacawiMosi Honeymoon Namid, silver torbie, and Honeymoon Nidaivi, brown torbie. Carolien Ossewaarde, Holland

CHAPTER 5
To Poly or Not to Poly

Kaleb with Behold What Faith Can Do PP, "Jaiden," blue tabby female. Phyllis Stiebens, Georgia, USA

The pedigreed Maine Coon cat described in this book can come with or without extra toes. A normal cat has five toes on her front paws and four toes on her back paws. A polydactyl cat can have as many as eight toes on each paw. The polydactyl Maine Coon is an interesting and loving pet, although not all cat lovers know about them. Having extra toes is a natural trait that was common in the beginning of this breed. Some people say that the beginning polydactyl Maine Coon cats were once about 40 percent of the population.

Polydactyl cats were thought to mouse better and to bring good luck. Having extra toes is a natural trait, not a deformity, and is a trait loved by many. Sailors, farmers and a few famous people adored the poly paw of any breed. America's twenty-sixth president, Teddy Roosevelt, had a polydactyl cat named Slippers. Author Ernest Hemmingway was famous for his love of cats with extra toes. Even now, more than half of the fifty cats at his estate have poly paws. Some are descended from his original cats, given to him by a sea captain. The story goes that sailors looking for sunken treasure believed six-toed cats were lucky and, thus, took the cats along. Hemmingway cats are not Maine Coons, but descended in a similar way to the lovely Maine Coon cat.

"I love my Mom!" Christele with Ari, silver torbie/white female. Christele Benoit, France

When the Maine Coon cat was a new registered breed and it came time to get them accepted at cat shows, the poly paw was removed from the breed standard in hopes of getting championship status sooner. Some of our original breeders, though, continued breeding these Maine Coons with extra toes. The poly paw was so treasured among Maine Coon breeders that polydactyl cats were allowed to be bred, even though they were not allowed championship status at shows. For many years, Maine Coon poly-paw cats have been shown in the Household Pet class. Often the polys were sold as pets while their non-poly siblings continued breeding and showing.

The love affair with the poly paw continued through the history of the Maine Coon cat, and it is still a very popular trait. You can see in pedigrees where polydactyl ancestors show up, because they often have a P or PP in their name. Typically, the P means poly on front only, and PP means poly on front *and* back. Many of our lovely worldwide Grand Champions are descended from poly ancestors. Many breeders want to keep polydactyl in their lines. They believe that kittens with normal paws from a polydactyl parent also inherit some of the heavier boning associated with this trait.

**"Yes I am loved!" Kylie with Behold Windows-of-Heaven Open PP, shell cameo female.
Phyllis Stiebens, Georgia, USA**

"My paws are bigger than yours!" Bloomingcoons Wynn PP, solid blue. Caroline Vergeer, Holland

In The International Cat Association (TICA), Maine Coon polys have been shown in the New Traits Class since 2005. As of May 1, 2015, the Maine Coon polydactyl can be shown in Championship in TICA as part of the newly formed Maine Coon breed group. We expect many beautiful poly-paw Maine Coons worldwide to be shown with great enthusiasm and pleasure. Since 2008, polys in the New Zeeland cat fancy may compete for Championship status along with the *normally* pawed Maine Coon cats. Cat Fanciers Federation (CFF) is presently working on accepting Maine Coon polys into championship status also, as is the Cat fanciers in Australia. So far, in Cat Fanciers Association (CFA), the poly paw can only be shown in the Household Pet category. Federation Internationale Feline (FIFe), a cat association in Europe, unfortunately banned polys from breeding and showing in 2013. Many European breeders refuse to give their poly-paw Maine Coon cats up. Polydactyl paw Maine Coons have been shown in Europe, just so judges can see this lovely trait. These judges have often remarked at the lovely boning, quality, and temperament of the polys shown to them.

There have been many recent scientific studies which all prove that having polydactyl paws is a harmless trait that causes no detrimental effect to the cat. The toes on polydactyl Maine Coon cats are pre-axial, which means that the extra digits are on the thumb side of the paw. They can have extra toes on one, two, three, or all four paws. The number of toes can vary from paw to paw, but the average is one or two extra toes per paw.

TLC Polycoons Karen K Narasaki P., Sharon Otten-Boult, Holland

TLC Polycoons Butch P Cassidy, Sharon Otten-Boult, Holland

Here are a few pictures of X-rays of poly feet where you can see the formation of a mitten paw with different toe formations. In one X-ray, the smaller toes seem to not be connected. These are called "dew claws," and the connection is by tendons. On the second X-ray, you see the dew claws connected by bones and joints. On a snowshoe foot, it appears that there is just an extra toe or two added to the paw. There seems to be no extra space between the toes, whereas with the mitten paw, a space appears. X-rays are not a necessity with polys, just a curiosity to better understand how the feet develop.

When looking at the paw to count the digits, it is important to look at the bottoms of the feet and take note of the paw pads, as well as the toes and nails. Knowing all of these factors makes it easy to determine if the poly's extra toes, thumbs, or dew claws create a certain paw formation. There are two types of paw formations: the mitten paw and snowshoe (or patty) paw.

The differences in the snowshoe and the mitten types are unique and worth mentioning.

The snowshoe poly paw (also called patty paw by some breeders) really makes *extra-large* paws and leg boning, which will make the Maine Coon look larger and more solid than he already is. Some breeders describe their boning as being like tree trunks. Watching a snowshoe-type paw reach into a water bowl and scoop up a drink is also a fun experience. When a normal paw Maine Coon runs around their home, they can make loud thumping noises as they run, slide, and jump. But when a snowshoe poly paw does the same thing, it appears the sounds are a bit muffed. It almost sounds like a cat wearing fuzzy slippers, and this too can be a really fun experience worth noting. Instead of *thump, thump, thump*, it sounds more like *swoosh, swoosh, swoosh*.

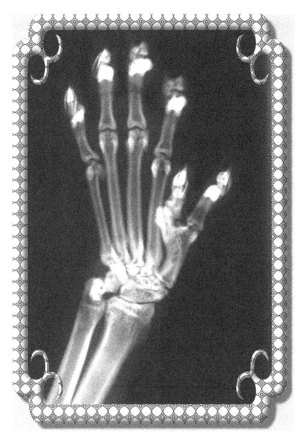

**X-ray of Janarc Ung Rico P of TLC Polycoons.
Sharon Otten Boult, Holland**

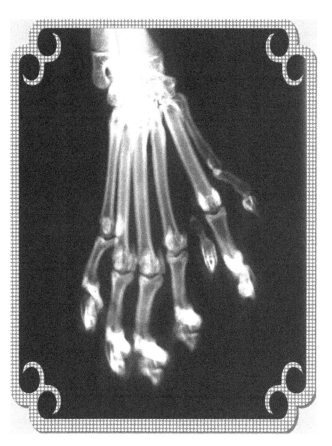

**X-ray of TLC Polycoons Karen K Narasaki P,
Sharon Otten-Boult, Holland**

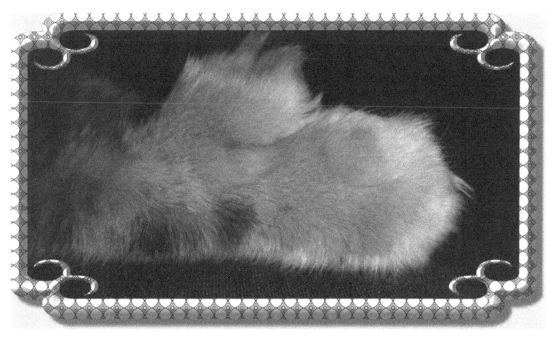

Mitten paw of Isatis Descoonsdelysane. Yanick Stocco, France

Snowshoe paw of Dynamicats Fireworks. Rianna Vande Vusse, Holland

The *Snowshoe* paw is a well-rounded row of toes next to each other forming a large paw with no distinct thumb.

The mitten-type paw can make a person smile, especially if the cat uses his paws as a hand with a thumb, as many of them do. Using a scratching post is very unique, as they use their "thumb" to hold the edge of the post or shelf. It sometimes appears the cat is part monkey, because of the way he uses his thumbs. While watching one walk toward you on a hard floor, he may not even appear to be a poly paw. The thumb toe is pointing toward the back, allowing you to see only four or five toes heading forward. It is when the cat pauses, and you see that extra "thumb" in the back, that you realize how unique those paws are. The *Mitten* paw is self-describing, it looks like a mitten with a thumb. This look is created by the extra digit(s). An example of this configuration is on a smaller dew claw and a thumb.

Prairiebaby Polly of Oticami, blue tabby female. Izabella and Robert Sijka, China

**Allegiance Love Lovely Lynx, Lord of hearts, and Legend of Toruk Makto, nine weeks old.
Elena Udovenko, Bulgaria**

Boonland's Lucky Strike P, brown tabby, seven weeks old. Marjan Boonen, Holland

Adelheids Haiku Ai PP and Adelheids Haruka Isa. Adela Kroupova, Czech Republic

Wackymoon Double Trouble P, red tabby male. Berit Sorensen, Denmark

Both types are happy healthy cats! The extra toes are fully functional. Sometimes, though, the extra toes cannot be stretched and their nails sharpened on a scratching post. Your job will be to watch these toenails and make sure you clip them so they do not grow long and hurt the cat.

Polydactyl toe formations are, in general, passed down from generation to generation. For example, a snowshoe poly parent usually produces snowshoe poly kittens, and mitten poly parents usually produce mitten poly kittens. Sometimes an additional toe on the mitten-type paw gives the impression of a snowshoe, because of the *lack of space* between the thumb and first toe. And sometimes the *lack of a toe* on a snowshoe poly paw appears to be mitten paw because of the space between thumb and first toe. When two polys of different paw formations are bred together, you can get poly formations of both types in the litter. Two cats of normal paw cannot make a poly paw kitten, as it is a dominant feature. This means the poly-paw feature cannot be carried and then show up later in normal paw parents. Whatever you think of poly paws, it is a personal preference about what one finds more attractive.

Kumskaka Gandolf the White P, white male. Phyllis Stiebens, Georgia, USA

Litter of Kumskaka snowshoe poly paw kittens, three months old. Phyllis Stiebens, Georgia, USA

When a person meets her first poly paw Maine Coon, it is typically a very exciting experience. Maine Coons are a large cat, with solid boning and paws already larger than normal. When you add just one extra toe or two per paw, the boning is even more substantial, the paws are larger, and the cat can really make quite the impression. The poly paw heightens the effect.

"See my big back toes?" Daddy Longtail Qu-ann PP, brown torbie w/white female. Anne Duguet, France

"Mine are prettiest," Daddy Longtail Rain PP, blue torbie female. Liesbeth van Bergen, Holland

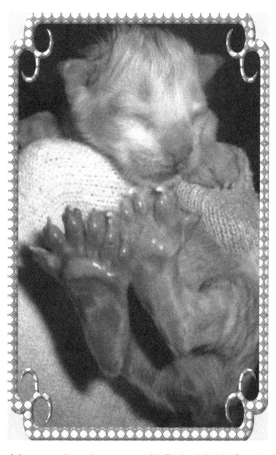

"Bet Mine will be bigger when I grow up!" Behold All God's Gifts PP, "Zane."
Phyllis Stiebens, Georgia, USA

**"I have cool front paws, can you see this?" Mrs. Paws Honeysuckle Baikey,
"Kymber," brown tabby female. Danielle Carroll, Georgia, USA**

Keep an eye on those big paws! The Maine Coon poly cat is around for a long road ahead. Many breeders and pet owners love them dearly and are not able to own just one. The Maine Coon cat has its own fan group, and once you own one, you will agree with the love affair.

**"Okay friends, let's end our a-paw-theosize times!" Furkats Kasie, brown tabby/white female.
Sue Nystrom, Arizona, USA**

CHAPTER 6
Your New Kitten

Sonshine's Michigan, white female, two weeks old. Danielle Carroll, Georgia, USA

If you have determined what color of cat you want to adopt and developed a relationship with a breeder or two, it is time to make the plans for getting your new baby. Besides deciding the color and gender, you will also want to decide the quality of the kitten you want to adopt. What is the difference, besides pricing, for a pet quality verses a show quality kitten?

Pacific, Picasso, and Portland, black smoke males, three months old. Izabella and Robert Sijka, China

**Triskel kittens: Flower, Sammy, Odeyssa, Sunset, Billy, Julio, and Elliot II, three months old.
Florence Salles, Quebec, Canada**

When looking at photos of Maine Coon kittens, you have to realize that the breeder sees much more than you do. You are looking for a good family member and may know when you see something you like. But why is that one, perhaps, more expensive than others? Quality for a pedigreed kitten depends on many factors. The breed standard is a written description for judges at shows to determine how well the particular cat fits this description. So this is the first area you would need to learn in order to know one quality verses another in purchasing a kitten. This is one reason it is important for breeders to show their cats for many years and learn what they are breeding properly. How tall are the ears? What is the distance of the ear set on top of head? How square is the muzzle? Is the chin weak or straight? Does the profile have the proper dip or is it straight? What is the body length and tail length? Do the eyes follow the proper shape and accepted colors? On top of all these standards to follow, how is the cat's personality? If the kitten has a shyness, skittishness, or total fear that the breeder does not think will be worked out through socializing, then this is a fault for a reduced price. The purchaser should be told truthfully about the quality of body, type, and personality so she will know she is buying what she is looking to buy. Some families do not mind a Maine Coon who is more shy and timid of new people and situations. This type of family would be what breeders look for if they get a kitten like this. There is also the size factor to consider in this breed. Maine Coons are large built cats and many people want a large and heavy set cat to join their family. This is something the breeder also considers when pricing their kittens. Most breeders do not actually set the price on any kitten until the kitten is approximately eight weeks of age or so. Even then it can be a good guess, as size and quality can wait and start showing up closer to sixteen weeks. But once a price is set, a good breeder will not increase the price, and may, in fact, lower it. For this reason, you may be told a higher price when the baby is little and then, by adoption time, the price may be less.

Heart of Maine Funky Footsy, black female. Petra Oosterbroek, Holland

"I am not into any trouble yet!" Peeta Mellark, male, six weeks old. Phyllis Stiebens, Georgia, USA

One thing to remember is that there is no perfect cat. We all strive to create better and better, but nature, as it is, always has one fault or another. Go in search for a kitten that you and your family will see as the perfect cat. Sometimes you will find a breeder who already has kittens ready to adopt. But often, you will find a breeder who has a litter coming, which might produce your dream baby. Being involved with the breeder and her family from the beginning will add to the excitement of the whole process. Do not rush into anything, and be patient with a breeder who may not be able to yet produce the perfect kitten for you. You will have a long-term relationship with your cat, so choose carefully and wisely.

When a female cat is bred, she will be pregnant for an average of nine weeks. Gestation for cats is typically fifty-nine to seventy days. Maine Coons seem to average sixty-five days. They have the natural instinct to take care delivering and raising new babies. Sometimes a first-timer, however, can get confused and have problems, unless humans are near to help her out. Babies can be born head first or breach with no problem either way. The new baby is born with a bag around its face, and the mama will remove this quickly with her tongue so the baby can breathe. Most breeders assist so as not to stress the babies, and to watch the joys of the birthing process. After the kitten is born, the mama continues to lick the baby dry and chews the cord, separating the baby from her body. Sometimes mama will grow weary from the birthing process, and the humans can then help wipe and dry the babies as needed, but this is not necessary for most litters. Breeders will often try to bottle feed, just in case the mama needs a little help. Kittens will not take any milk if they are getting enough from mom. Most breeders will weigh kittens weekly and keep track of their weight to make sure each kitten is growing as he should. Babies grow at an amazing rate, and the group will soon be larger than the poor mama cat. Because of the stress on the mom, many breeders will start the babies eating on a plate of soupy foods. This is the beginning of growing up. Ask your breeder for photos during this time so you can enjoy "growing up with your new cat."

Maine Coon babies grow quickly but have much maturing to do each week of their young lives. The whole world can be scary at times, too overwhelmingly curious at others. If you are able to get photos from your breeder, you will be amused to see them learning their world! The learning continues when you bring them home too, so keep a camera handy at all times.

Behold kittens playing with finger shadows. "Mad Hatter," cream mackerel tabby male, and "Iracebeth," blue mackerel tabby female, three months old. Phyllis Stiebens, Georgia, USA

Clover with Behold Gandolf the Grey, silver tabby male. John Webb, Delaware, USA

Remember not to get in a hurry for your kitten to arrive at your home. To become a well-adjusted feline, they need handling from their human and cat families. While looking at baby photos from the breeders, try to imagine what this tiny little baby will look like as an adult. Choose the male or female for your special family pet and, as the breeder will require, put down the necessary deposit, which will hold your baby for you while you wait for him to grow old enough to come to your home. Before you take possession of the baby, though, there are a few things for you to do to get ready for him.

"You wanted to use this?" Dynamicats Songs for Polar Bear, white male, and Dynamicats Crack the Shutters, silver tabby/white male, seven weeks old. Kitty van Ewijk, Holland

The first thing is to kitten-proof your home. This is similar to baby proofing your home, but you will not need gates at your doorways (if you use them, the kitten will just jump over them). Try to imagine, while looking around, what could be fun (and dangerous) for a kitten. Loose electrical cords and window blinds are the first thing you need to tape up, bind, or hide. Since kittens like to touch things—and that includes with their mouths—look out for anything poisonous. All household plants need to be hung up high or removed from the area where the cats will be allowed, or at least for a few months while the kittens are younger. Although many plants and flowers are not toxic (some are, so be careful), they will not look so pretty once they have been molested, dug at, and chewed on a few times. If you have a kitten who really likes plants and does everything he can to get into them, you might want to consider growing some cat oat grass for them. They can chew it, lay in it, and just have fun with it.

"It fell over by itself!" Samanta Parent Pride, torti/white female. Elena Korobkov, Russia

"I am innocent!" Behold When Angels Sing of Coonjunction, silver torbie female. Karen Milder, Texas, USA

"Do not disturb until breakfast," Behold Duke Kahanamoku Ali'I, silver tabby male, two years old.
Lisa Pakosh, Bahamas

Where is the baby going to sleep? Many people say they want the kitten to have full run of their home from the start. That is fine, but not always a good way to start out with a new kitten. When you bring home your kitten, he may be a little fearful, and it helps relieve the stress if he's put into one room where he can adjust. There are new smells, noises, and people (and maybe animals?) for him to adjust to. By giving him just one room with sleeping quarters, litter box, scratching post, water bowl, and toys, he can adjust to the new things sooner. Visit his first room often and let the kitten get used to your voice, your scent, and your touch. You will be the one he will lean on the most and become their mama, so be patient if the kitten is afraid of you to begin with. Handle him gently and with great affection, and you will steal that kitten's heart. When you are not present in his room, he will need something to play with. Most babies come from litters of many siblings and are used to a crowd. Your new kitty will be fine when he has his human littermates around but, when alone, the baby can get bored, depressed, or in trouble (or all of those). After a day or two have passed and you see the kitten is eating and using the litter box with no problems, then you may open the door and allow the cat more access to the house. Buying a box or bed for him to sleep in can be fun for you and the kitten. Most likely, though, if given the choice, he will choose your bed and your blankets as his favorite snuggle place.

There is much for your new kitten to adjust to. He will respond happily and easily if you are patient. Be careful when introducing him to new animals, though, whether cat or dog. Protect your baby until he feels welcome in the home, and he will bond well with the other animals, in time.

A scratching post is an essential to training, as well as having a fun place to get up high and look out windows. Many cats also enjoy napping on their posts. Having toys available in the cat's room is a good idea, but do not leave anything there they can eat. Leave nothing with thin plastic or rubber, and nothing that tears or has feathers or tassels. When you are around to monitor them, any toy is fine. Even children's toys can be great fun for them to play with. Toys made of wood or plastic and not of small pieces can provide much added entertainment. They are especially fun, though, if a child is playing with them at the same time. While you are there to watch, you can allow him to investigate all over, but during his first week or so, keep a good eye on him to watch if there may be a hazard that he has found and you have not. It is usually a good idea, also, to have extra litter boxes around the home. A baby is a baby, and he may forget where he last saw a litter box.

"I love this bed you gave me, Mom!" Juapaka Caia, blue-silver torbie/white, two years old.
Jutta Kiehn, Germany

"We love this playground!" Vanitosa Del Sole Nero and Vitbria Del Sole Nero,
blue cream/white females, odd-eyed. Ennio Spanu, Italy

"We love the Barbie playground so much." Amy with Nikov, Jag, and Simon.
Carolien Ossewaarde, Holland

"I am already a winner, sis, let's get on with our game." Lindsay with Cuban Rose,
nine weeks old. Cassandra de Greef, Belgium

"I know you will be here soon Mom!" Sir Mordred Los Miticos, blue/white male, nine months old. Sabina Ostermann, Spain

We recommend that you put your kitten in the room he is used to when you are at work, if there is nobody else to watch him. This is necessary only for a couple months, as you train him to be a good kitty and he learns what is and what is not allowed. Once he has a general idea of the rules, you can leave him loose all the time. He will learn to sit in a window and watch for your return. If he has an outdoor area to play in while you are gone, he will be watching for you from anywhere he wants. If you are gone a long time, be ready for some serious affection.

"Waiting for Mama." Versus Imagine, Viktoria, and Oasis. Radka Vacikova, Czech Republic

"Hugs and Kisses." Marcia with Bajacoon Angelina Bellucci, calico, five months old.
Marcia Oliveira, Brazil

If your kitten has any adjustment issues when he has been in your home a few days, always contact the breeder. Remember, she was the mama of your kitten first and can help you get everything working in harmony. Once your baby has adjusted to your home and family, as well as your routine, you can enjoy the loving times to the maximum. Turn those times into training times, and your baby will enjoy all he is learning. If you have a cat or dog in the house already, they and your new cat will become great friends in no time at all. If you have children that live in the home or visit your home, they too will bond with the kitten. They will build a unique relationship with each other, and you will see some very fun antics happen. Whether they just sit together or snuggle in the cutest ways, it will be a bonding for both child and kitten. Kittens do funny things and some will nuzzle, kiss, or even suck on your child's clothing or hair. You cannot stage a show between them, it will just happen. Maine Coons, like children, like to be the center of attention and affection. Give them what they need and they will bloom right before your eyes. Just have fun and watch your baby grow and mature into a spectacular Maine Coon cat. The more you include the baby in your daily life, the happier the kitten will be. A happy kitten will truly reward you with a lot of love and devotion. Just include all family members in the kitten's life.

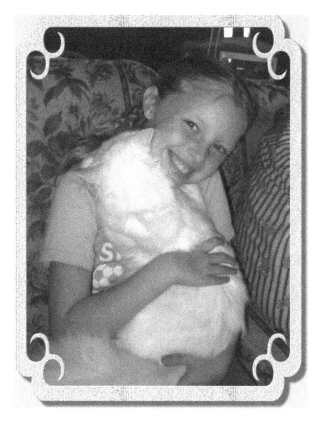

"Sucking hair is my thing, ummmm." Kylie with Kumskaka Princess Bubbles PP, white female, two years old. Katrina Nager, Florida, USA

Now what are you going to name your baby? Breeders usually keep the registration papers for a pet until you neuter or spay. Sometimes though, they will give you the registration papers at purchase time. The item "not for breeding" is marked on the slip. Whenever you get your papers, you need to figure out a unique name for your kitty. Even if you call him something very common, like Fluffy, the *registered* name should be special and unique. Since there are millions of cat names in the computers of the cat registries, you may have your first name choice denied, if it is too much like another cat's name.

Kumskaka Princess Bubbles PP in her Castle, white female, one year old. Katrina Nager, Florida, USA

A person can also be unique in choosing a special photographic name for their kitten. If you were to do this, then be creative, and photograph in that particular theme. Here are two photos that give some simple ideas of such creativeness. You can just photograph your kitten in a particular background as the owner of Princess Bubbles did, or you can use a scrapbook computer-program to create a very specific page like Bumblebee's family chose to do.

**Kelimcoons Bumblebee in her collage. Torti/white female, eight weeks old.
Sandra Tassinari, Massachusetts, USA**

There are endless ideas for names, and we will attempt to get you started. Here are some theme ideas that might just fit your little mister or mistress.

- What is your favorite movie? If it's a long movie, like my favorite, *The Lord of the Rings,* then you would have an endless supply of name ideas. You could have the name of Lord Celeborn, Samwise Gamgee, or maybe Lady Eowyn. Or how about a place name like Fangorn Forest or a building like Minas Tirith? What is your favorite book? You can name your kitten after the lady in distress or maybe the charming prince. Similar to the movie idea above, you could name your kitten after a character or place you love to read about, like *The Hobbit,* or the main character, Bilbo Baggins. The Bible is one of my favorites. There are endless names, especially for boys. But even in pretty Bible verses you can find a suitable name. One of our females, for instance, was named "In the Twinkling of an Eye" and we called her Twinkle.
- What type of music do you like? You can call a kitten after a favorite group or some pretty poetic words from a song that steals your heart. Name your kitten from something you love!
- You can name your kitten after real people you admire or who impress you. You can be creative with the name, making it more fun too. We liked Rush Limbaugh, so we once named a cat Rush Coonbaugh and called him Hudson, which is the real Rush Limbaugh's middle name.
- Do you like reading or hearing about the galaxy? God made a pretty impressive world out there, and so much of it is almost poetical in title. Look at your books and maps of this lovely outer world and maybe call your cat Whirlpool Galaxy or Cassiopeia. You can just have fun with something as similar as Comet or Red Mars.
- Foods may have a special meaning to you also. Something like Chocolate Mousse, Praline Pecan, or Peanut Brittle can be enjoyable. Sometimes kids can have more fun with this than we adults, and I often hear of very cute names for Maine Coons this way. Names like Crouton, Carbonated Colors, and Cheesepuff are all very unique and fun.
- Animals or bugs can be fun also. Praying Mantis (call him Manny), Monarch, Cheetah, Loon, Moose, or Grizzly can be fitting names.
- Get out some history books and have fun looking at those. American names for an American cat are rather fitting. You can have Paul Revere or maybe a famous general from the Civil War. Perhaps even a historical figure shown in a DVD movie, like Wyatt Earp or General Armstrong Custer. Nobody said you have to choose the hero of such a movie; you can always choose a character that just steals your eye—or heart. In the DVD of Gettysburg, I love J. Lawrence Chamberlain (who was actually from Maine!).
- Native American books can be good sources of names and have meanings besides. Or use your ancestry: look up names of your ancestors and choose one you admire greatly.
- If your kitten has funny antics or enjoys unusual places in your home, consider naming her creatively from this. For instance, a cat who curls up in a bowl could be called Stone Soup or even Super Bowl.

The ideas are endless. Use your imagination and name your baby what you want to call him. Some people just get online or get a baby-name book and pick a child's name for their baby Maine Coon. There are lovely names, and it could take you a long time to find the right one, but keep looking. Maybe you want to have a Logan in the family or an Emmett, a Matilda or maybe a Tess.

As your baby grows up, keep taking photos. You will be amused at the antics and funny poses. When they settle into a funny place, grab your camera. You will be surprised at how fast they mature and change in looks, so photos will help you remember those changes over time. Use your own camera and a nice clean background, and decorate and snap away. Or even go to a professional and watch the poses of your baby. Keep up your kitty photography!

Phyllis Stiebens

**"You do not see me . . . I am not available." Charming Lynx Ilvy-May, torti/white, one year old.
Michaela Peham, Austria**

"Do we match yet?" Mo & Co's On the Cover, calico female. Monique Zweers-Daams, Holland

84

"Thanks, Dad, just what I wanted!" Oticami Morgan, red tabby/white male, three months old.
Izabella and Robert Sijka, China

CHAPTER 7
Training Your Gentle Giant

Indigo of Coonquistador, red silver male, one year old. Anna Krylova, Russia

Training a cat can be very fun with this breed. Maine Coons are smart cats and can, many times, end up training us. They also seem to have a sense of humor, which makes training more fun. Since some cats automatically have special ideas about what fun is, each cat will be different to train. With games, for instance, some will fetch a thrown toy or piece of paper and bring it back to you. Others may grab a toy and then run off with it, hiding it for you to find. You may even have a cat who does not care for your idea of toys, but will find his own toys (and not always to your liking). It is up to you then to get to know your cat and start the training from there.

"I want so I take!" Kumskaka Lady Galadriel PP of Tuftsntails, shaded cameo female.
Sue Riley, Michigan, USA

"She may be small but is my best friend!" Kambrie with Leaena Special Agent DiNozzo, "Tony," red tabby male, two years old. Katrina Nager, Florida, USA

There are many types of training. The main category we will talk about here the most, is training the *do*s and *don't*s of the home. Other training we will not get into much include training for tricks, agility (and, yes, cats can be and are trained in such things), and filming. Cats, with persistence from their owner, can be trained for most anything you can imagine. The trick to getting the most success is persistence on your part. Cats are not like dogs, who will do most anything to get your approval. A cat just seems to think he deserves the approval. Your relationship is one of shared affection. Why try to earn it like a dog does? So, go about training as you would a child and keep at it. Be firm but have fun. Cats like a life of ease and enjoyment, so if you get mad at them, they will just avoid that area of their life that causes any stress. One of the most important training techniques for your Maine Coon is to handle him: Hold him, carry him, throw him over your shoulder, and stretch him out in the air. When you get children involved, it is even better. Kids have a different voice and quicker movements, which really can help get your cat used to more of his world.

A rule to follow with your kitten is this: Whatever you want your Maine Coon to do and not to do when he is a very large adult, you will need to teach him as a kitten. It's all as simple as this! You really do not want to handle a twenty-two-pound cat who suddenly has to be bathed and has never had a bath before. Believe me, you will wish you had included bathing as part of his childhood training. When he is a kitten, just start the training and add anything you need as you go along. Your relationship with your kitten will grow as you do more and more with him. Even if they do not like what the training subject is about, they will learn who the boss is (to a point). They will love you for spending that time with them.

Kissan Tiedot Chatvallon Royal Caroline, silver torbie female. Jarno Pyykko, Finland

Nascat Turbo Charged, silver mackerel tabby/white. Donna Hinton, Texas, USA

Fion Ewe Diesel von Thivoedone, white. Netty Schipper, Holland

Do you want to travel with your cats? Get them used to noises, people, bright lights, and moving objects (like a wheelchair). Get a soft travel carrier and take them for short trips to the pet store to start out. Take them in the car or put them in a wagon for a little trip down the road. The point is, get them where there are new things and new noises and keep them safe. They will learn to do it all in stride. Do you want your cat to enjoy visitors in your home, show affection to him as he does to you? Then have visitors over often while the kitten is young. Ask neighbor kids to visit on occasion to play with the kitten. Have friends over for dinner and TV and just let the cat hear and smell and notice what is going on. Life will become part of a normal life. Many cats grow to love the action on the TV screen, and it can be difficult to actually see the screen if you have more than one Maine Coon.

Do you want your Maine Coon to visit nursing homes, hospital wards, 4-H groups, or other social situations? Start getting them used to the world out there, and they will learn that it is all a normal part of life. They will need to be of a relaxed nature, and not all cats will fit this personality. If yours does, then get them used to strangers handling them and a lot of noises that could startle them, so eventually strangers and noises won't stress them out. The calmer the cat, the more often you will be asked back with your cat.

Behold Our Lord Reins, "Oliver," white male. Tory Bombard, Florida, USA

If you have an interest in showing your cat in cat shows, then the cat must be bathed and groomed often. Clipping claws, combing, using hair dryers, and other various handling techniques will all be needed in order to get a cat who relaxes and takes a cat show in stride. They will also need to get used to a large area where sounds echo and wheelchairs or strollers can squeak going past them, with babies crying or children yelling. In any plans you have for your cat, just think ahead and get started. Your cat will adjust if you do it slowly and keep at it. Do you want your cat to share the great outdoors with you? If you do not have a secure fenced in yard or area for them that is safe, then your kitten must learn to wear a harness. We see many cats just take this as a part of normal life, although the first few times many cats wear a harness, they may lie down, as if dead, and refuse to get up and walk. This is a temporary situation and nothing to worry about. The cats learn quickly that the harness is simply a part of their apparel and they can do more things with it on and will eventually look forward to wearing it. Maine Coon cats love to play outside and grab at bugs and fluttering leaves and walk in the garden, checking out everything with you. They will not mind a romp in the snow or in the hot summer breezes. Some people will attach a leash to the harness and hook it to a clothesline outside and let the cat stroll an area on its own.

Orion Romeo, "Herus," blue tabby male. Beth Ferreira, Brazil

People can entertain, garden, or just relax, and all the while the cat is part of it all. Just make sure he is wearing a snug fitting harness that he cannot get off if he panics. Some cats are even trained to swim in the family swimming pool while the family swims. Some cats do not like it and yet others beg to go in again and again. A swimming cat is fun to watch. They keep their ears down, so as not to fill with water, and put gusto into the swim to the side. Think they are done? Nope, many jump right back in. This breed seems to have a fearlessness of water and it may in part be due to the soft quality of their coats, which are partially waterproof. You will need to feel the texture of this coat to truly know its quality. Is it winter, and the cats cannot play in the water outdoors? Do not worry, they truly love water, even if they slide around on it. So do not be afraid to try new things with your cat, and if the first time really scares him, just take it slower and try again later. You will know if you see interest to pursue or if it's just not something your cat ever wants to do again. Do not scare your cat by keeping at something of which he is very afraid. You can get seriously hurt while the cat is seriously afraid/stressed.

Vision, Firechief, Tibbitt, Pierre and Viper. Pia Jensen, Denmark

Dutchsweetloves Ringo, red tabby male. Angelique Eeltink, Holland

One type of training your cat will need to learn is not to scratch what you do not allow him to be scratching. Maine Coons cannot be declawed, so it is up to you to continue the scratching post training that your breeder has started. The cats learn very well, so make sure you have a post ready when you bring that baby home. Some cats prefer carpet, others like wood, and some like rope, so, to be on the safe side, try to get a post that has all three types of scratching material on it. The post should be tall, since these cats love to look down on their world, but even a short post will keep their interest for a while. There are even silly cardboard scratching boxes you can buy. Many cats will shred those in days, they like them so much. One of your easiest training tools will be a water squirt bottle. When your kitten scratches the carpet, couch, or some piece of furniture he is not allowed to mess with, squirt water at him and say no. Then take him to his post and pet him and praise him while he is on the post. It does not take long for them to realize what is required. These cats do love water, but they really do not like to be squirted with it.

Los Miticos Little Tenderness, Living Los Vegas and Los Miticos Hit the Road Jack. Sabina Ostermann, Spain

Luigi Tsunami, brown tabby male. Stefania Arici, Italy

If you want your cat to stay off the counter or top of an antique dresser, for example, try to think of how to make it an unpleasant experience. For instance, you might want to put empty pop cans on a dresser. One trip up, the cans fall and make a racket, and the cat will find another place that is more to his liking. A little discipline and a lot of love and patience always pay off. Do all you can and never give up. Anything of value takes a bit of work. Be creative and smarter than your cat. If you find he has a fascination with something you do not want him involved in, then put your thinking cap on and try to outsmart him in his antics.

"This one is mine!" Samotna Gwiazda of Shedoros, brown tabby/white male. Dorothea Scibura, Germany

Phyllis Stiebens

"Like this Mom?" Grandeur Cosmos Prince Paris, brown tabby. Heather Barnetson, Ontario, Canada

I will tell you a little story about one unsuccessful training time we had, as not all training goes as planned. The only thing we were *unable* to train our cats away from was our little birds. We had cages of canaries and finches. When the cats would not stay off the stands or cages, we hung the cages from the ceiling. We made the mistake of thinking the birds were then safe. One of our girls learned that she could jump upon top of the refrigerator and then leap onto a birdcage. For a while, the cages held up, but it sure scared the poor birds. We began covering the top of the refrigerator with baking pans, cookie sheets, and such. It only took one leap up there during this time to keep the cat down—while the pans were in place. You would not believe the noise from all those pans falling onto a ceramic-tile kitchen floor! However, she then learned to watch for when the pans were not up there. It did not look pretty for visitors, and sometimes we actually used those pans to cook with. One day, we left for town when the pans were down. We had forgotten about the cat getting on the refrigerator. We never saw it happen but, when we returned, the bird cages were all on the floor. Without going into details, I will just say we no longer had any little birds. We were creative and able to teach our cats many things they could and could not do, but we could not fight nature in this one. The instinct for the cat with the birds was stronger than her desire to keep us happy. Now that the birds are no longer in our home, there have been no more problems with training.

We did train one cat, by accident, in a way we did not mean to. It involved those silly birds again. During one cat's attempt to get at the birds, I used our broom to reach up and try to sweep the cat off the top of the refrigerator. The broom worked and the cat jumped down and took off, but was afraid of that broom from then on. I would sometimes forget and go about sweeping the tile floor of the kitchen, and she would take off. For a while we could not figure out what was going on. When I saw her make a big circle to walk around a standing broom along the wall, eyeing it carefully, I then realized that she was afraid of that broom. I guess I was the slow one to learn here. Keeping *that* girl away from the birds was easy. I just leaned the broom on the front of the refrigerator, and she would not even get close to those birds!

96

While doing your daily training with your cat, be sure to involve children. Kids have a zany way of seeing life and can often teach the cat much more in their own way. They have a special way to hold, in game or in affection, and kittens learn early on to respect that young person. We do not know how they know, but cats automatically seem to know when a human is a child and are more careful not to injure them.

"I think she likes me!" Kambrie with Behold the Meaning of Life, "Duckie". Phyllis Stiebens, Georgia, USA

Ravagnani Silverado 89th, "Gandolf," silver tabby/white male. Adriana Marcelo Ravagnani, Brazil

The main thing to remember about this lovely breed of cat is that they love their human family with a strong bond. Like any cat though, nature will sometimes supersede you, and you will have to be very creative in your training. Sometimes you may fail at the training but other times you will succeed greatly. Just don't give in. A spoiled, untrained cat is about as attractive and fun as a spoiled-brat child. A little discipline and a lot of love and patience always pay off. Do all you can and never just give up. Anything of value takes a bit of work. Have fun and make memories while you are with your Maine Coon, but don't forget to let the cat have a break. Fun and work, or training, can wear out your sweetie. Watch them fall asleep right in the middle of it!

Daddy Longtail Emma, white female. Liesbeth van Bergen, Holland

CHAPTER 8

Maine Coon Grooming Basics

Aukje with Mt Kathadin's Kane, brown tabby/white male, fourteen years old. Dorien Baaijens, Holland

Grooming is never hard on this breed, but it can be work, nonetheless. There are many parts to the grooming process, and we will briefly highlight each one here. If you are not showing, then bathing your cat may be just for emergencies.

Grooming your cat should be a part of his loving. Every Maine Coon should be groomed, although not every Maine Coon needs to be bathed. Get in the habit of the grooming part, and when a bath is needed, the cat will be used to much of the process already. Every night, for instance, comb him as he lies across your lap. Although he does not need grooming this often, doing so will associate the grooming times in his mind as loving times. Your hands are a good loose hair remover, so use them to your benefit. Pet like crazy, and let your cat feel very safe and loved. Then put the comb in your hand and continue with the stroking. Comb in the direction of the fur growth, and just keep going back over the area until it is silky, right to the skin. If you find a mat, just pull gently. If it will not come out, get a scissors and trim carefully. When the coat is nice and silky and combed out, run the slicker brush over the body and ruff carefully. This will often take off the lighter, shedding layer and give it a finished look. We like to use the slicker brush on the tail next, and fluff that up nicely. If used gently (so as not to scratch the skin), it works also for the little mats that can show up around the sides of the ears. Combing a lot, especially in the dry winter months, can create static in the fur, and the cat will not enjoy his love grooming. A dryer sheet (a used one, as a new one will put oil on the fur) rubbed on the fur will help. A little Static Guard sprayed on your comb will work also. Sometimes we even like to use the spray-on hair conditioners for humans during this time. Since they do not use oils, they do not make the cat's coat greasy.

Some cats of this breed sport an oilier coat and thus look prettier when the oil is removed. Some pet people use a spray-on dry shampoo. I have not found one I liked too well, however. I always preferred to bathe my Maine Coon to get them nice and shiny. If you have no plans to show your cat, just bathe him when he is extra oily or has gotten into something that makes him dirty. There may even be an occasion when your cat gets a skin problem (like ringworm), and bathing will help it clear up faster. A vet can be helpful with shampoos for your cat's particular skin dermatology problem. Some long-term breeders can also be helpful informing you about things that work and do not work.

**"Now this is the life for us!" Radka with Williamina Amadeus and Gale by Imagine Glamour, red males.
Radka Vacikova, Czech Republic**

Gather some supplies and get your work area all set up. Grooming tools (combs, nail clippers, etc.) should be easy to get to at bath time. As cats become more used to the bathing routine, you can teach them to sit or lay on your lap for the pre-bathing and post-bathing times. Until they are used to it all, we do recommend a carrier to be used while getting them used to a hair dryer.

For basic grooming, you need some supplies:

- A few good quality, metal-tooth combs
- A fine-wire, gentle slicker brush
- A nail clipper
- A couple of basic shampoos
- A degreaser that is safe for cats, like Dawn Dish Soap (without any added items for soft hands or germ killer) or Goop Hand Cleaner (do not get the ones with lanolin or grit added)
- A cup for rinsing
- Lots of thirsty towels
- A cat carrier
- A fairly quiet hair dryer
- Some cats need a coat conditioner and/or a coat thickener

For show grooming, you may need some extra supplies:

- Color enhancing shampoo
- Texturizer shampoo
- Cream rinse
- Texturizer spray
- Static spray or wipe

Bathing is easy if your cat is used to it. Most breeders will start kittens on bathing, and it will be up to you to continue this training as they mature. You do not want to have a huge Maine Coon who needs a bath but wants to take a pint of blood from you simply because you want to bathe him. Remember that whatever a cat is used to, he will not fight against. Just as dog people need to socialize a dog while young, you need to do the same for your Maine Coon cat. Whatever you want him to do as an adult, get him used to as a kitten. Some cats even enjoy a bath and look forward to it all—combing, stroking, rubbing, and petting are enjoyable to your Maine Coon. If they are having nothing to do with it, just give them a little break and then start again. They will get the hint.

"I am ready Mom." Leon, red/white male, eight years old. Diana Heckel, Germany

101

"Already been washed, don't mess with reload." Alberto Tomba Canary Hunter, brown mackerel tabby male. Signe Heering, Denmark

Routine non-show bathing does not need to take a lot of time or work. Have all your supplies laid out. Some people use a bathtub, others a sink, and some still have other ideas for the perfect bathing facility. We use our kitchen sink for youngsters, which is divided into two compartments. Once the cat is a full-mature size, however, the sink no longer works well, and then we use a walk-in shower or a laundry tub.

Once the cat is combed and the claws on front and back are all trimmed down, you are ready. We recommend that before you start your bathing session, have a love fest first. Get your big baby happy and well loved. Once he is snuggling all over you, it is time! When we bathe a youngster in our sink, we fill the sink half full, rather than running too much water. A Maine Coon coat has natural oil and the water will generally run right off. This is where your first shampoo comes in. Dish soap, hand cleaner, or something similar, is your first item. Make sure this soap does not have lanolin in it, or any harsh abrasives. Put the soap on your hand and gently rub down the body, lightly. Do not put much on, or your rinsing stage will last too long. You are not actually *cleaning* the cat here, but *removing the oil* so the shampoos will then clean them gently and nicely. Part the fur on various areas of the body. Is it wet clear to the skin? If not, you are not ready to proceed. Once you have the cat thoroughly soaked, you are ready to start the shampoo.

"Ahh, that is very nice, thank you!" Mt Kathadin's Kane, brown tabby/white male. Dorien Baaijens, Holland

"No, not that area, it's private!" Gunnar and Gentlecoon's Frankdandy, red tabby male,
two years old. Magdalena Karlsson, Sweden

"Hey this is fun, more water here!" Felinafolia Chris Rock, red tabby/white male.
Josiane Boing Mulberstedt, Brazil

"I like it better up here, thanks anyway." Heart of Maine Join My Voodoo, brown torbie female.
Petra Oosterbroek, Holland

Do not ever pour water over the cat's head. Keep the face and ears free of the water and use a wet, squeezed-out washcloth to clean this area, which we will speak of later. If water gets into the ears, it can create an ear infection, which you do not want. And water in the eyes can burn, since it may have shampoo residue in it. During your whole bathing process, keep the cat's head dry.

The first shampoo is usually a flea shampoo. A flea or medicated shampoo usually requires five minutes (or more) to soak on the cat before you can rinse. Having a helper during this part can be very beneficial. Even if your cat has no fleas that you know of and the skin is nice and healthy, it is usually a good idea to use a flea shampoo for step one. It does not hurt and can be a good cleanser to start with. Many flea shampoos can be soothing to the cat's skin. Once you have shampooed the cat all over and started the countdown, keep the cat happy with gentle talk or massaging the neck. When the timing is done, it is time to rinse. I have seen many people who ended up with a dirtier looking cat when finished than when they started. Why? Because the cat was not rinsed well. Any soap residue will not be good for the cat (who is going to lick it) or for the fur, since it will drag it down. Rinse and rinse and rinse again. If you are not showing or doing extensive photography sessions, you can stop washing now. Many times, however, shampooing at least once more can really make a difference in how nice your cat will look.

"Brrr, let me snuggle a bit please." Anura Family Stars, torti female. Oxana Abdulkhakova, Russia

If you want another step added to your cat's beauty bath, you can use a cat shampoo for a specific color or a nice human shampoo. There are many cat color shampoos that can help make his bath a total success. A bluing shampoo for white cats really makes their pure white sparkle. Browns do well with a bronzing shampoo, and solid blacks look good with a black on black shampoo color. You can make mistakes, but as long as you are not bathing for a show, your mistakes will be learning tools. For instance, if you buy a shampoo for a red color fur and your cat has a lot of white on him, the white color can become pink. Some shampoos tend to bleed, so just practice and see the end result to know what is best. You can also ask show breeders for their advice on the different color shampoos. Bathing your cat often will help you learn what shampoo works the best for your cat. Many show people will keep their shampoo list a secret, so you may have to learn your own. If, for your last step you prefer a human shampoo, use one without conditioners in it so you do not end up with a cat greasier at the end of the bath than at the start. A good brand to look for is Pert without any conditioners.

For the actual bathing, it can be beneficial to have an extra pair of hands to help out. Maine Coons that are used to their owners and household noises are pretty easy going about anything, like bathing, that the human family wants to do. Be careful not to scare your cat during bathing or she will not be easy-going and tolerant of baths.

When you are at the end of your bathing, the last step is to rinse. It can help to have extra water to float the coat a bit and really get all residues out of the coat. Some people like to use a conditioner now. If you are showing, if your cat has a static coat (winter heat time?), or if your cat has a coat that tangles easily, then a cream rinse might be something to try. Do not put it on the tail, however, since all your rinsing automatically puts everything down onto the tail. So use a tiny bit on the sides, front, and britches (the longer hair on the upper rear area of the legs). Then rinse well. When there are no more bubbles or any film to your rinse water, you are done with this part.

Once the water is gone, and before you go to the grooming and drying steps, you have a few little hands-on things to do. Maine Coons are known for greasy ears, and so the wet, squeezed-out washcloth can wipe out the oiliness and they will be nice looking really fast. The face area does not need any more work than this, but if your washcloth is clean (no soap residue) you can wipe over the cat's facial areas and remove any eye dirt, nose dirt, and any oils. Lift your cat onto a thick dry towel and lay another one over his back. It is time to proceed to the grooming part.

"Come on, Mom, don't mess with that area at all." Stoneocean Natchez, brown tabby male. Kitty and Dominic Van Ewijk, Holland

Do not *rub* the cat with the towel, as you do not want to tangle the fur. Once the cat is done dripping, set the cat on a clean dry towel and begin to slowly comb out the wet fur. Do it slowly and gently and in the direction of growth. Do not comb the tail while wet, as it can pull the hair out, and it takes a long time to grow back. Next, turn on a hair dryer. If your cat has had this done before, he will accept it with no problem. If he is not used to it, the best plan is to put him in a cat carrier and hold the dryer at the door. Keep taking him out to comb and fluff the hair that is drying.

"Warmest spot in this home!" Cover Girl of Coonjunction, brown tabby female. Karen Milder, Texas, USA

Some Maine Coon cats look better if allowed to air dry from this point on. Others will not look nice at all, so you will need to experiment on your cat to see how his coat looks done each way. On some, do not let the fur dry on its own or it will get tangles as well as little curls on the belly and britches, which can mat. On others, the coat air dries and lays nicely and beautifully along the body. We prefer, for most of our Maine Coons, to dry them as they sit on our lap, and we can comb, lifting legs, neck, and back end. Once again, it can be easier if you have an extra pair of hands from a helper. When the cat is mostly dry, you can let him run loose. Sometimes they dry faster when walking around. A nice warm area for this time is fun, and a photograph might be worth snapping. Sometimes the cat will relax in an out-of-reach area, and this is your first opportunity for a unique photograph.

"I am coming down when I am good and ready." Kumskaka Billy Graham, cream tabby/white male. Phyllis Stiebens, Georgia, USA

We have found that many cats think they can do a better job of grooming than you can and will lick themselves dry. A little hairball ointment *before* bath time might be a good idea for this reason. A bath will often loosen hair on the body, and the cats appear to shed more. Actually, the bath helps remove the older hair that is going to fall out anyhow. Just comb a lot over the next few days and it will stop shedding the fur. You will probably need to clean your cat's favorite napping spot for this reason and a wire slicker brush works good for this.

Take a look at this photo.

Gold eye white female, "Tinkerbell." Phyllis Stiebens, Georgia, USA

Whites can be a little extra difficult to get bathed properly, but they can also be very sparkly when done. If you look closely at Tinkerbell in the picture above, do you see the dirt that was forgotten? Yes, her coat is white and combed and nice looking. For bathing just for home or photos, she is pretty well done. But if you wanted to show, then she is NOT done. Do you see the grime in her nose? The grease in her ears? The little bit of dirt at the edge of her eyes? These things will not be tolerated in a show and can take away from your overall scoring. So keep an eye on the little things, in addition to a clean, floating coat. It can make all the difference.

Once your cat is bathed and dried, let him relax a bit. He will be so clean and sparkly, that this is a good time to take your photographs. Find an uncluttered background and remove any cat hair and debris and get out the camera. With a feather stick toy, get your finely groomed feline to enjoy some games. Find some funny poses, or get the cat dressed in puppy or doll clothes. This can be a real annoyance for the cat, but great fun for your family. Whatever type of photograph you want to take, just enjoy it and don't make the session too long. Your friendly feline can be like a toddler and will grow weary of the sessions if they are lasting too long. Over the next few days, take as many photos of your baby as you want and get many photos to show his creative personality as well as his beauty. You can also have your cat professionally photographed, which can be a real joy to have hanging on your wall. Your Maine Coon will change a lot over the years with maturity, so keep taking the photographs. Photos of a fun and vibrant kitten will bring back many memories when your feline has grown old and slower and you remember how much you love this cat.

"Yes you are allowed to admire us!" Triskel Coco, red tabby/white male, and Triskel Chanel, brown torbie/white female, two months old. Florence Salles, Quebec, Canada

"Baby grooming is not so bad!" Sitalas Daylight of Kajaphis, blue tabby. Kathrin Eingruber, Germany

**"Please tell me I do not look like her dolly!" Kumskaka Eternity Choice, "Brynn," silver tabby female.
Phyllis Stiebens, Georgia, USA**

CHAPTER 9
What Should I Feed?

Jukon of Kitty-Crazy, silver tabby/white male. Elisa Schneider, Germany

Phyllis Stiebens

Like any feline, the Maine Coon cat was created by God as a carnivore. This simply means they were made to eat meat. Not cooked, like you and me, but raw and fresh. We live in a time, however, where people are busy and prefer to make everything easier and faster. So now there are many products on the market to check into for your convenience. Your Maine Coon will be a large cat and needs a nutritive diet. There are many things you can feed your cat, but not all of them will be the best for him. So where do we start?

"I just keep waiting. They will come soon." Oticami Gismo, cream tabby. Izabella and Robert Sijka, China

When you bring your kitten home, feed him what he was used to at his breeder's home if possible. As few changes to his diet as possible will help him adjust better. You can change it soon, but not right away. The digestive system is fragile, and any sudden changes will give your kitten runny stools and possibly make him vomit. The time of day for meals should also stay similar.

There are many foods for cats on the market. Processed foods are full of fillers, chemicals, and preservatives, though, and it is *your* job to look closely at the labels. Whether you feed dry, canned, or raw, it is up to you, the owner, to find the best. You can ask advice of others, but don't rely on just one person. Sometimes a breeder, friend, or even a vet will feed what is cheapest and easiest to feed. You will want to invest in your Maine Coon's future, and what he eats is a determining factor in his lifespan and health. Research online, read websites of food companies and look up the ingredients listed in their food. If you do not like what you read, mark that one off your list. Asking advice just gives you a starting point.

"This meal is mine kid!" Sitalas Daylight of Kajaphis, blue tabby. Kathrin Eingruber, Germany

"This is where they keep all the meat, so I have to check it out!" World Flower of Secret Schatz, brown tabby. Esther Guggenbuhl, Switzerland

**"I love this kid! One more please?" Emma, feeding Sandy, brown torbie female, six months.
Fieke van Schoten, Holland**

If you plan to feed dry foods, then you must comparison shop. There are so many bad fillers out there, and you have to find a food that is not loaded with them. Read all labels well before buying. Just because a label on the food you buy says "all natural," or "organic," or even "human-grade ingredients," you cannot really be sure what your cat is being fed. Sometimes only a tiny amount of something good is added and then the food is labeled as nutritious. Not long ago, cats and dogs were dying of kidney failure due to contaminated fillers from China. Some of the fillers were actually from plastic manufacturing, allowed in animal feeds by the Association of American Feed Control Officials (AAFCO).

On many websites you will be able to learn a great deal about what goes into pet food. From looking at many, we have found much information you may not like to read. We read where under the Food and Drug Administration regulations, only about 50 percent of a cow, for instance, can be sold for human consumption. The hide, bones, digestive system and its contents, brain, feces, udders, and various other undesirable parts are all left over after a cow is slaughtered and butchered. The stuff that can't even go into hotdogs gets consolidated and shipped to rendering plants. Slaughterhouses that handle pigs and chickens also send their leftovers to rendering plants. So do many other facilities that find themselves with large volumes of otherwise unusable dead animal parts, including animal shelters and veterinary clinics that euthanize a lot of animals. A rendering plant has a huge grinder that is filled up with whatever comes in. Some rendering plants are pickier than others, and some process ingredients in different batches to comply with state or local laws. But it appears most tend to dump in whatever they receive and start the grinder when it is full: parts from slaughterhouses, whole carcasses of diseased animals, cats and dogs from shelters, zoo animals, road kill, and expired meat from grocery store shelves (tossed in fully packaged, complete with plastic wrap and Styrofoam). This material is slowly pulverized into one big blend of dead stuff and meat packaging. It is then transferred into a vat where it is heated for hours to between 220–270 degrees F. At such high temperatures, the fat and grease float to the top along with any fat-soluble compounds or solids that get mixed up with them. Most viruses and bacteria are killed. The fat can then be skimmed off, packaged, and renamed. Most of this material is called "meat and bone meal." It can be used in livestock feed, pet food, or fertilizer. It joins a long list of ingredients that you might prefer not to see in your pet's food.

Here is a short list that shows some of the *approved* ingredients that you may not know about.

- Polyethylene roughage replacement (plastic)
- Peanut hulls
- Ground almond shells
- Hydrolyzed hair, poultry feathers, and leather meal
- Undried, processed, animal-waste products
- The following website explains all the long word ingredients in processed pet foods: http://www. dogfoodproject.com/index.php?page=badingredients

Something you will need to remember is that essentially there is no federal enforcement of standards for the contents of pet food. Technically the FDA has authority, but the agency has passed this off to a set of partnerships and nongovernmental organizations that encourage mostly voluntary compliance with the few federal standards. The AAFCO takes the lead in setting and maintaining standards, but it conducts no testing of food and has no enforcement authority. In practical terms, regulation of the contents of pet food is largely accomplished by those individual states that bother to get involved. Some states, such as Florida and Nevada, have no regulations at all. Others, such as California, require that rendered pets (euthanized pets from animal shelters) be labeled as "dry rendered tankage" rather than meat and bone meal. However, even California allows rendered pets to be processed and sold out of state for pet food as meat and bone meal. The city of Los Angeles alone sends about two-hundred tons of dead pets to a rendering plant each month. There is no inspection of pet food or meat and bone meal shipped in from other states.

"Don't get much better than this!" Kajaphis Einstein, cream. Kathrin Eingrueber, Germany

If you choose to feed dry or canned processed foods, that is up to you, but understand that a long-term, junk-food diet will have its effects on your cat's life. Feeding dry food is easier to feed, and some cats crave it and refuse to eat anything else. Feeding part dry and part raw may work as one solution. Learn your cat and find something healthy he will eat and enjoy. We recommend that you give raw meat at least weekly to help supplement a processed diet. Variety in a diet is always a good thing, especially when it involves feeding raw healthy meats. Once you do some serious reading on dry and canned processed foods, we feel you will agree that feeding raw is the best.

"Jump with me, come on!" Meekocoons Sandy, brown tabby female. Pia Jensen, Denmark

One option, used greatly in Europe, is to feed dead chicks. The cats love them and will get all meat/organ/bone in their meal. The Maine Coon will eat chicks as meals, snacks, or even dessert. Eating should not be a boring time for a cat. Grab your camera and watch the action. The cats have great fun playing with their catch. It is a natural food for a feline, so let them enjoy it.

If you decide to feed your Maine Coon a raw meat mix diet, you must find a place where you can buy your food. The meat cannot be just the ground flesh, like you find in a grocery store. Since the cat is a carnivore, they digest raw foods very well. However, they do not eat just flesh/meat. They also eat the bones, organs, brains, and sometimes some of the skin, fur, and feathers. Raw meat is becoming a very large industry for pet owners, and many companies are getting into this market. Go online and look around. However, you also have to be careful with online sources. Since this can be a large moneymaker, some companies are adding fillers, such as vegetables, grains and other things. There are email groups, like BARF (which stands for "bones are real food"), that you can join online to read and chat with other members for help. Many have recipes for their mixes, and all are different, which is good. Try not to feed your cat the same thing all the time. If you choose to feed raw meat as the sole source of your cat's diet, change the recipe and type of meat weekly or monthly. For those who can ship or have meats delivered, buy a variety. Goat, rabbit, turkey or chicken, lamb, beef, and sometimes duck or pheasant are all available from many companies. They grind flesh, bone, organs, and sometimes fur (in the case of some rabbit). Mix it in larger batches to save time later if you want, but it is best to sometimes add fresh powdered Taurine and fish oil just before feeding.

"It can fly, it can fly!" Dynamicats PP Fireworks, "Toby." Rianne Vande Vusse, Holland

"Don't bother me, crunch crunch" Wackymoon Rebel, odd eye white. Berit Sorensen, Denmark

"This one is mine." Wackymoon cats. Berit Sorensen, Denmark

We used to buy our meats in a coarsely ground mixture, with the bones and organs all ground in for us, but then we lost our supplier. So we started to buy ground meat made for humans—finely ground— and then mixed it with a proper vitamin mix powder. We use Feline Instincts powder and mix it with the ground meats, salmon oil, and liver powder and feed this daily. Changing the meat types is good, as well as giving treats of meat with bones. For instance, once a week we feed chicken winglets, chicken necks, stew beef chunks, or cut up chicken thighs. Everyone can decide for themselves how they want to feed their Maine Coon. Variety in types of food and vitamins can be a good idea. Just be careful with the cat's digestive system. Some will have zero problems, and others will not be able to change their diets often, if at all. Here is an example of a meal rotation of raw feeding that you may choose for a week, or one week changes, one month changes and so forth.

Monday: Cut up chicken thighs and remove the skin and the large bone in the thigh. All other bones are best left for the cat to chew on and work for his meal. Chicken wings can also be a good item here, but leave the skin on for those.

Tuesday: Chicken necks to chew on. (This is good for one day a week, but, to be fed more often, you will need to add some things to it, since it has very little flesh and no organs or vitamins). Turkey necks are too large to feed them, so you would have to do a lot of cutting or grinding to use those. If you have access to dead chicks, these would be good to add here for treats, although chicks are nutritious enough to be fed alone.

Wednesday: Ground goat with bone and organ.

Thursday: Ground turkey from grocery store, plus the Feline Instincts powder mix and salmon oil.

Friday: Ground beef and chicken from grocery store, plus the Feline Instincts powder mix and salmon oil.

Saturday: Ground rabbit and lamb with bone and organ. Most of our cats hate lamb, but we found that if you add ground rabbit, they will eat most anything. Rabbit is the best meal for felines, but it can also be one of the most expensive.

Sunday: Ground turkey with bone and organ. Adding some ground beef heart adds nutrition, as does powdered Taurine, Lysine, and Vitamin C.

"This is mine?" Luigi Tsunami, brown tabby male. Stefania Arici, Italy

"Hey, your food tastes better, um!" Lynette with Behold's Bebe. Blayne Saucier, California, USA

Phyllis Stiebens

"Please let me taste, okay?" Zettai Karen, brown torbie/white. Elena Korobkova, Russia

Blessing and Purdy helping mix the raw meat. Katrina Nager, Florida, USA

Do you want your cat to eat before you leave for work and again when you get home? Or do you want your cat to eat when your family eats? Although your cat may have his own ideas for when to eat, you can get him used to your schedule with some time and patience. When your family eats, your cat will want to join in, but be careful. Feeding cooked human food is not a good idea, not even as a treat. A human treat (meat) once in a while is not deadly, but hard to resist. When you have that sweet furry critter doing his best to get a bite, it is hard to resist. Give in once, and then give in again, and pretty soon, you are feeding cooked human food they should not have. They do have their own idea of what looks good, and some cats will make you laugh at what they try to get into. Eating any type of meat is a normal desire, but some cats may go for some very strange foods. I have heard cat people talk about their cats craving watermelon, lettuce leaves, pickles, and other strange items. Although it may be fun to share, it is best you do not put that in their feline body. Some things are good for humans, but are poison for cats, so research this. Onion, for instance, is a great human food—raw or cooked—but it can make a feline very ill. Just keep raw meat treats or some cat treats around to keep your feline happy. Have fun taking photos of your felines, however, when they try to steal your food. This can be a very fun photo session (on your part anyhow).

Dry, canned, raw, chicks, or any other type of meat that may arise, what you feed your cat is your choice. Just do your homework and do your best. Your cat will reward you for your research and hard work in getting him the best food possible, by living as long as he is able. Maine Coons average fifteen to eighteen years, with many living into their early twenties. Loving your Maine Coon is shown in many ways, so do not forget to research their foods. They are depending on you.

**"You going to open any of this now?" Brunelle Dzikosc Serca, torti/white female.
Izabela Grabysal, Poland**

121

"Do not disturb me, Mom will be right back." Figa Akord of Shedoros, brown torbie. Dorothea Scibura, Germany

"Eating what comes natural." Sweetloves Onyx, brown tabby female. Angelique Eeltink, Holland

CHAPTER 10
Health Care Responsibility

Leigh Ann at McDuffie Animal Hospital, Thomson Georgia. Phyllis Stiebens, Georgia, USA

The Maine Coon is a hardy breed of cat, but it is not immune to all problems. Buying a kitten from a reputable breeder who tests his lines for genetic and health problems can help. You, as the owner, also have things to do to maintain a healthy kitten. Feeding a proper nutritious diet is one step, as mentioned in Chapter 9, but there are other ways for you to keep your cat doing his best.

Grandeur Baby Ruach with Dr. Catherine Went, DVM, cameo tabby male. Heather Barnetson, Ontario, Canada

Vaccinations

Getting a kitten with vaccinations is important. All cats, including Maine Coon cats, need to be vaccinated. The breeder will start your kitten with a couple of kitten vaccinations. The basic three in one or four in one vaccinations are needed for the first year. One or two kitten shots and then a booster at about the age of one year is typical. Many vets, breeders, and pet owners are stopping vaccinating at a year of age, feeling the risks outweigh the benefits. A proper immune system is important, but some cats do not do well with the additives used in vaccines. You can read many articles online to find that cats are being over-vaccinated. The results of this are tumors, cancers, and early deaths. Many veterinarians now say that one vaccination lasts for seven to fifteen years, and, if this is the case, why are we vaccinating yearly?

Some vaccinations, like rabies, are required by the state or for traveling. If required, then do the shots. If not required, then decide for yourself if you want to proceed with the shots. Do not be pressured by your vet or friends if you feel the shots are unsafe for your cat.

If your cat is going to be indoors 100 percent of the time, then some vaccines are not worth the risk. You may choose to do them anyway, but read up on them first. There may come new vaccines on the horizon, which also should be used carefully. We remember when feline infectious peritonitis (FIP) was prevalent, so a nasal vaccine was made, and every cat owner was pressured to use it. Many cats actually died of this virus, and the experts finally seemed to pull it away from vet offices. There are scary viruses out there, and we hope more vaccines become available to protect our felines, but sometimes the risks are just too high to try them for a while. Watch others and learn. Then make your choices.

Ruby with Dr. Lauren Sanderlin DVM. Phyllis Stiebens, Georgia, USA

Vet Care

Micro-chipping is a good idea for your cat. It has nothing to do with health, but rather vet care. Should you allow your cat outdoors, or if he is an escape artist, then this might be worthwhile. If lost, this can sometimes help you get your cat back. A micro-chip is a small electronic chip that is put under the skin of the back of the neck of a cat or dog. Any animal control officer, animal shelter, or veterinarian will be able to scan the micro-chip which will bring up the contact information for the animal. This is one way to prove ownership if your pet ever gets loose and someone else tries to claim him.

Los Miticos Hit the Road Jack, black/white, thirteen weeks old. Sabina Ostermann, Spain

Los Miticos Living Los Vegas, cream tabby/white, thirteen weeks old. Sabina Ostermann, Spain

Keep your cat updated on all stool checks and worming. Internal parasites, such as roundworms, and external parasites, like fleas, must be treated to keep your cat healthy. Your vet can tell you what treatment to use, but you can also look online. Talk to others and find out what works best for them. You mainly need to know what parasite you are dealing with, and a stool check at the vet office can tell you. Sometimes, though, you will *not* need a stool check. There may be occasion where the cat will vomit and you will see long, skinny, spaghetti-type worms in the vomit. These are roundworms, and you can call your vet for the proper wormer. If you see your cat with what looks like little grains of rice wiggling around his anus, then your cat has tapeworms. Tapeworms come from fleas, so keeping the fleas gone will help keep this parasite out of your cat's body.

For fleas, the easiest thing on the market, is the monthly flea drops. There are a few types and you squeeze a small container on back of your cats neck (where he cannot reach it) every four weeks. Some can now be bought at a pet store and others have to be bought at a vet office.

Behold Stuart Minion, blue male, four months old. Phyllis Stiebens, Georgia, USA

Cleanliness

Cleanliness is a first on your list. Keeping your cat and his environment clean will keep many bacteria and germs away. Soap and water will be your best cleaning supply, but bleach is sometimes needed.

For the cat's body, make sure his feet, britches, and tail area are not soiled with feces. If it happens (and it does), clean him up. Also clean any places where he went walking.

For the cat's supplies, everything must be kept clean. Wash his food and water bowls weekly, daily if they eat wet or raw foods. Wash their bedding and toys every so often, as they pick up dirt and germs also. The litter box takes the most work and needs daily care. Clay litters absorb urine and thus become a smelly environment for any germ. Clumping litter makes it easier to remove all liquid and solid waste, and thus most odors, and is preferred. Scoop as often as you can, and then remove waste away from people and pets. Since most litter boxes are made of plastic, they will need a good scrubbing weekly. If your cat is healthy and does not make a mess with loose stools, etc., then the box can go a couple weeks before a good scrubbing is needed. If your cat gets sick, the litter box will need to be cleaned right away.

Wearing rubber gloves, scrub the box with a hot, soapy solution and then rinse. Then soak the box in a bleach-water solution. It is a good idea to have more than one litter box for use during these times. Many Maine Coons love to get into what you are doing, so watch the soapy or bleach water bucket, if you wash the litter box in their presence.

Covered litter boxes keep the cat's mess more confined. Some cats do not prefer them, however, and you may have to try a couple to see which they like best. In addition, some Maine Coon cats are too large to move around properly in a covered box. You do not want to make it inconvenient for your cat to use a litter box. One family built a wood furniture cabinet in which to keep their litter box. It had an open end by which the cat could enter and leave. The family loved this, as it kept the smell and mess confined, even in their family room. Some companies now sell similar box covers.

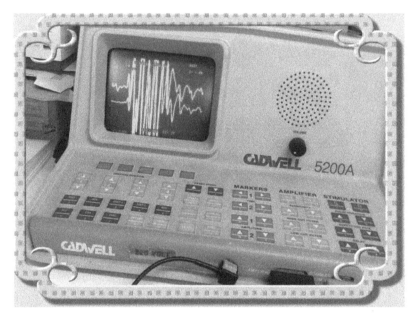

BAER test for hearing. Wavy lines mean hearing and straight lines mean deaf. Petra Oosterbroek, Holland

Health Testing

If you buy your kitten from a reputable breeder, you will be buying a kitten with some testing and no known genetic problems in his line. There are a few genetic tests currently, and there will be many more in the future. Some tests help learn what health problems are *not* in the cat's parents and lineage, like

- PKD (polycystic kidney disease): This is a disease in which a large number of fluid-filled cysts form within the kidneys and are present from birth in affected cats, but they start off very small. It is inherited as an autosomal dominant trait so its full name is autosomal dominant polycystic kidney disease (AD-PKD). This disease needs an ultrasound so the vet can look for cysts on the kidneys. If there are none, then the cat is negative for the disease. If cysts are found on the kidneys, then this cat will die young from kidney failure. There is no cure.
- HD (hip dysplasia): This takes an x-ray of the hips, which is sent to the Orthopedic Foundation for Animals. It is the same as with dogs. Most cats do not go lame the way dogs do, but they can have pain, especially in older age. This x-ray will tell you if the ball of the hip bone

is well into the socket area. If it is loose or completely out, then there can be pain for the cat as he matures and grows. An OFA rating that shows no HD can be listed as mild, good or excellent.

- HCM: (Hypertrophic Cardiomyopathy): This disease is where one chamber of the heart gets extra thick and eventually stops working, causing heart failure. There is a DNA version of this test, which tests for one gene that may be associated with this disease. The most important test, however, for this disease is a heart ultrasound. The best ultrasound to look at the heart is a color Doppler. Parts of the heart are measured and thicknesses are looked at. At one year of age, the first test should be done. It is a very young age to have this test, but it can be useful. It eliminates a cat for breeding that has early HCM and thus can be removed from the breeding program or can be started on proper medication to have a longer life. The test at one year of age is also a good idea to give the cardiologist a starting heart measurement. The test should be redone every couple of years up to about five years of age. If no obvious HCM signs are seen, the cardiologist can look to see if there are changes in heart measurement and see if this cat might be at risk. If so, they will need to be retested more often.

Heart of Maine Kitty Tatoo having BAER test, white, eight weeks old. Petra Oosterbroek, Holland

There are many DNA tests and more to come. One day we all hope for tests that can be done to say for sure if a cat will or will not get a particular problem. Until then, just keep researching everything you can. A test of any kind does not provide a 100 percent guarantee in this world, however. Nothing is yet perfect or foolproof. It can, nonetheless, give you peace of mind to know your feline is tested.

Gentlecoon's Frank Dandy, cream tabby male, fourteen months old. Magdalena Karlsson, Sweden

Safety

Keeping your kitten safe means work on your part. Having your home kitten-proofed is a good start. Watching and training are important daily chores. But there may be other ways listed on your contract to keep him safe. Keeping him indoors or in a safe outdoor environment is an important part of his safety. Having plenty for the cat to climb on and play with will make him very happy. They need exercise, like we do. The outdoors has many threatening and deadly things in it, and you, as the parent, must protect your cat from them. Most cats are totally fine to be indoors, in their human world. If never allowed outside to play or walk on leash, they will normally be afraid to venture out. Keeping him indoors will prevent him from being exposed to diseases carried by feral cats, wild animals, traveling dogs, etc. This is just one less stress he will have to try to live through and keeps you happy also.

Some people want their cats outside with them and are willing to provide a safe environment. Cats of all kinds will love this and enjoy the extra big play area. Wind can provide much extra play toys with grasses, trees, bugs and much more. Wiggly bugs on the sidewalk can entertain them for hours. As long as the playground for your cat is safe from his escape or another animal's entry, you can have a great deal of enjoyment watching and interacting with your Maine Coon in the great outdoors.

Feed a good diet, keep vet care and health testing updated, keep in protected area, and he will do very well if just a happy loved cat. Just being part of his human family will keep him thriving. Play with him often, love with him daily, and make him a true member of your family. Keeping this lovely breed entertained is not really so very hard to do. Open your world to him and watch his creativity bloom! Enjoy and watch your Maine Coon cat thrive.

Ladylike Atomic Actroy, Blue tabby male, four years old. Ellie Kruithof, Holland

Lily, Mac, Merlin, and Rupert. Louise Davie, Scotland

**Jade and Ruby with Hannah and Dr. Lauren Sanderlin, McDuffie Animal Hospital.
Phyllis Stiebens, Georgia, USA**

Hawkwind Maverick, brown tabby male, one year old. Magdalena Karlsson, Sweden

Below is a list of websites where you'll find useful information.

- The Winn Feline Foundation, www.winnfelinehealth.org winn@winnfelinehealth.org
- Morris Animal Foundation, www.morrisanimalfoundation.org mailbox@morrisanimalfoundation.org
- Cornell University, http://www.vet.cornell.edu/fhc/
- UC Davis, Veterinary Genetics Laboratory, http://www.vgl.ucdavis.edu/lyons/catphir.php
- Recent Press Releases to keep up on news for all companion animals from Zoetis, a global animal health company dedicated to supporting customers and their businesses in ever better ways: http://news.zoetis.com/press-release/cats/zoetis-and-winn-feline-foundation-announce-call-research-proposals

Behold the Glory of the Lord, "Brina," brown torbie female, eight weeks old. Phyllis Stiebens, Georgia, USA

Kaleb with Bubbles and Kylie with Nate. Katrina Nager, Florida, USA

Nori and Naomi, three months old. Gosia Zeszutek, Poland

CHAPTER 11
Pre-Genetics of Color 101

Oticami Rock, Oticami Rusty, and Oticami Rossman, brown classic tabbies. Izabella and Robert Sijka, China

135

What is the genetic color make-up of your Maine Coon cat? To learn actual genetics, you will need to take a college class, so do not think that this is what you are getting here. This chapter is simply to enjoy learning a few basic things about how your kitten got its sex and color.

The sex-determining factor of genetics is the same for cats as it is for humans. A male is **XY** and a female is **XX**. A female can only give an **X** to each baby, so it is not up to her to determine the sex of her children. The male is the one who does this. If the male puts an **X** on a baby, it is a female. If there is a **Y**, then it is a male.

Now let us add coloring to this very same issue. For a cat, the girl babies get an **X** from both parents, remember? Well, the **X** gene carries color, but the **Y** does not. Hence, a girl can get two color genes—calicos, tortoiseshells, and such. A boy gets his **X** color gene from mama and his **Y** sex gene from daddy. This will help you figure out how the boy kitties get their coloring from mama. Yes, the dad's other color genetics can influence the ending color that baby boy gets (like smoking, solid, dilute, etc.), but he cannot put the actual color on his sons.

Tikasi kittens, nine weeks old. Anastasia Goloveyko, Russia

For those of you who know zero about color genetics, you may be surprised to learn that there are just two color genes in the cat world. Before you call me a liar and wonder where I got such information, keep reading.

BLACK and RED. That is all there is. Cats do not get just one color gene, or we would not have the variety we have. A long string of genes is added to the individual color code that makes a cat's coloring. There are genes that change coloring shades, genes that make a tabby pattern, genes that add smoke, genes that eliminate all color, genes that add color-point, and the list goes on.

Genes come in pairs: one from each parent. Some genes are dominant and some are recessive. We use capital letters to show a dominant gene and a small case letter to show a recessive gene. First, the Maine Coon is a longhair, and that is recessive. **L** is for shorthair and **l** is for longhair. They cannot carry a shorthair dominant gene to be a longhair cat, so the gene list starts out as **ll**.

Remember that the X gene is female and carries color, and the Y gene is male and does not carry color. A red female would be **XrXr**, and a black female is **XbXb**. And since a female can be two colors, she would be **XbXr** for a tortoiseshell. A red male would be **XrY**, and a black male would be **XbY**.

136

Royals of Maine Fairytale, torti female. Marianne Verschuden, Belgium

Stordire's Firestorm Blaze, red tabby male. Ramona Valentine, Colorado, USA

For our example, let's start out with a black male, longhair, **llXbY.**

Sonshine's Pure Chaos, black male. Danielle Carroll, Georgia, USA

A black Maine Coon cat is changed by adding a tabby (agouti) gene. **A** is agouti (tabby), and **a** is non-agouti (solid). Tabby is dominant and solid black is recessive. So let's say one parent put tabby on, and one parent put solid on this cat. Now you have a brown tabby male, longhair, that carries the solid gene. So far, you have **ll XbY Aa**.

Bestseller Bahrain, brown tabby/white male. Nataliya Karpova, Russia

But what pattern? Mackerel pattern (the stripes down the body) is dominant, and that is a **T**. The classic pattern is recessive, which is the blotched pattern you see on many show cats, and that is a **t**. Some breeds even have a *ticked* tabby pattern like the Abyssinian cat, which is **Ta**. This gene was not in the original Maine Coon gene pool, but has been added recently. We will not mention it in our tabby genetics here, however. If dad is a Mackerel tabby and carries the classic, we know all his kids will be mackerel tabby patterns if he throws the **T**, but can be classic if he throws the **t** and his **t** is accompanied by another classic gene from mama. So, for our diagram, we will say that our brown tabby boy got the classic recessive gene from both parents, so now he is a brown classic tabby male, longhair, who carries the non-agouti (solid) gene. He would be described this way: **ll XbY Aa tt**.

How do we get the lovely blue tabbies we see out there? (Gray color tabbies are called blue). Since blue is a recessive gene, it can only be passed down by a blue cat or one who carries blue. Non-Dilute is **D**, dilute is **d**. For our brown tabby to become a blue tabby, both dilute genes have to be given, but if only one is passed down, then he stays a brown tabby that carries the blue. We will not change the cat into this for our diagram, but a blue tabby is a diluted brown tabby. And, although they look different, genetically they are almost the same.

Blue tabby female. Heather Barnetson, Ontario, Canada

So let us say our brown classic tabby cat now carries solid and dilute and is longhair and male. We then have an **ll XbY Aa tt Dd**.

As a pet owner, you may not care about what genes your cat carries, but this can help you figure out how your cat came to be a color that, perhaps, the parents were not. For instance, how did that breeder make such a pretty silver tabby? The silver gene, **I**, can only come from a silver parent. Meaning, two brown tabbies cannot make a silver tabby (or any other non-silver colored cats). There are no recessives in the silver gene. If the cat got one **I** gene for silver, he is a silver tabby. If he did not, he stays a brown tabby. For breeders, this can get even more fun. If the cat gets one **I** gene for silver and one **i** gene for non-silver, he would be called heterozygous for silver. This means simply that he is a silver tabby and can throw silver babies *or* non-silver babies if he is used for breeding. If he has two silver genes (from two silver parents only), he would become homozygous for silver, which means he can *only* throw silvered kittens.

Sweetloves Indy, silver tabby male. Angelique Eeltink, Holland

This silver gene turns a brown tabby into a silver tabby, a blue tabby into a blue-silver tabby, a red or cream tabby into a cameo tabby, and a solid color into a smoke. The silver gene also comes in variants, but that will not be explained here. I mention it only because many people ask why the silver tabbies can be so different. You can get a silver tabby in light or dark silver as well as a shaded (pale) silver tabby. The shaded silver cat just has more of the smoking on the fur follicles making whiter coloring against the skin than the color tipping on the ends of the hair shaft. They are very attractive and desirable cats, but for now we will go with a regular, darker-silver tabby. So now our example of the longhaired, brown classic-tabby male that carries solid and dilute just became a silver cat with one silver gene. His list is now **ll XbY Aa tt Dd Ii.**

How about that solid white? This may surprise you, but, genetically, a white is a colored cat. It may be the silver classic-tabby gene list we are making here now, but with the added **W** for solid white. All that this gene does is cover up all the colors so they cannot be seen.

Kumskaka Bilagaana of Shedoros, "Billy," white male. Dorothea Scibura, Germany

Solid white cannot be carried as a recessive trait; it can only be passed down from a solid white parent. It is the same as the silver gene. If this cat gets one **W** for white, he becomes a heterozygous white cat. The white gene cannot be carried since it is dominant. If both parents give a **W**, he would be a homozygous white cat. Since white cats can have deaf babies, it is *never* a good thing to breed white to white, therefore, pretty much there is no such thing as a homozygous white cat. To end our genetic list, we have a silver, classic-tabby longhair male who carries dilute and solid and is now a solid white. He would be described this way: **ll Xby Aa tt Dd Ii Ww**

Many solid white kittens are born with a color spot on top of its head. If not too big, the color spot will disappear as the cat grows, but it is very useful to a breeder. You may never know the exact color your white cat is masking, however, unless he was bred. But it is fun, anyhow, to see the little colored peek-hole on the head of a kitten.

Here are some general rules for color genetics: to get a dilute color, both parents must carry the dilute gene or be a dilute color. Therefore, the dilute of solid black is solid blue, of brown tabby is blue tabby, of red tabby is cream tabby, and of silver tabby is blue-silver tabby. To get a solid color, both parents must carry the solid gene or be solid. The only way to get a silver tabby or smoked variety is if one or both parents is a silver or smoke. The only way to get a solid white variety is if one parent is a solid white. Kittens with white, without white, and the amounts of white (including the van colored cats) also have genes added to the color gene list. We did not mention any of those here but will make one simple note. Two cats *without white* cannot make kittens *with white* (except for white spots called lockets and those are not able to be shown as a locket is a disqualification). But two cats *with white* can and do make kittens with *no white*, and that is because the *without white* can be carried if relatives are without white.

Here is a little quiz to help you see what you are learning. Simple color genetics:

Q: If your cat is a blue mackerel tabby, can his parents both be brown classic tabbies?

Behold PP Show Me Your Ways Lord, "Shjon," blue mackerel tabby female. Phyllis Stiebens, Georgia, USA

A: No. Do you know why? Mackerel tabby is the dominant gene, so a dominate pattern cannot come out of two recessive genes. If one parent is mackerel and one is classic, then the answer here would be yes.

Also, in same question: Can two brown tabbies make a litter of blue tabbies? The answer here is yes. If both carry the recessive dilute gene, then they can make dilute blue tabby kittens.

Q: If your cat is a silver tabby, can one parent be a black smoke and one parent be a brown tabby?

**Jersey, Rocky, Dallas, Charlie and Kitty of Shadowlady,
four months old. Corry Venema, Holland**

A: Yes. The reason here is that the smoke is actually a silver, but is a solid silver instead of a tabby silver. In this case, your cat would carry solid since one parent was a solid.

Q: If a red tabby male is bred to a brown tabby female, can they make red tabby sons?

Tikasi litter, nine weeks old. Anastasia Goloveyko, Russia

A: No. The part to remember here is that the boy babies get their color from mom, not dad. Dad makes them a boy and can make them a dilute or solid or smoke, but not a red tabby. If mom is not a red tabby or part red tabby (like a calico), then there can never be a red son born to her, no matter the color of the dad. Here is more what you would get from this mating: brown tabby boys and brown torbie females. A very common and exciting color mix!

Family Value Babies: April, Ace, Angelique, Ariel, Apollon, and Abigail. Angela Fomicheva, Latvia

Q: If a solid white cat is bred to a brown tabby cat, can they have a whole litter of brown tabbies?

Novuelle Nastia, Novuelle Jour, Novuelle Univers and Novuelle Mattin. Alena Mosna, Slovakia

A: Yes. The white is masking a color and perhaps it is a brown tabby underneath the white. Each white cat can produce a different number of solid white kids per litter. One litter may have zero whites and one may have all whites, like this one.

Q: If a litter of kittens is born with 100 percent boys, does it mean the dad threw all X genes or Y genes?

Triskel litter, brown tabby/white. Florence Salles, Quebec, Canada

A: The answer here would be all Y genes. The boys have one X from mom (for color) and one Y from dad (for gender).

Q: If a solid black male is bred to a calico colored female, what percentage of tabbies would be born to this mix?

Greengrove babies: Layak Ravi, Lari Malari, Lahar Nirav, Laboni Maya, and Lalima Niyat.
Marcin Skwarczynski, Poland

A: None. Solid black is solid and recessive, and calico is solid and recessive. Two recessives make all recessive colors. The kittens would be 100 percent solids, although blue can occur if both parents carry the dilute gene also. Just one note on this photo, a red tabby can be a solid red, but to the untrained eye, it looks like a tabby. Just so you know, if two solids are the colors of the parents, the red kitten is not a red tabby but a red solid, even with the tabby markings showing up.

Q: What are the colors of sons the brown tabby male and red tabby female can have? Think about this: If a brown tabby male who carries dilute and solid is bred to a red tabby female who carries dilute and solid.

Abygail, Aileen, Alive, Andkicking, and Awakenings. Jacqueline Dol, Holland

A: Mom is a red tabby, so all her sons will be red tabby or the dilute version, called cream tabby. There can be solid versions of the red and cream, but, to the untrained eye, they will all look like tabbies in red or cream.

Q: What are the colors of daughters the same two parents can have?

A: Girls are a mix of colors, so all of them will have red with the darker tabby. If dad passes brown tabby, girls will be brown patched tabbies. If he throws dilute of brown (blue tabby) and mom throws dilute of red (cream tabby), the girls will be blue patched tabbies. If both parents pass down solid but not dilute, you get torti females. What is really fun is if both parents throw solid and dilute, you then get very pretty blue torties, sometimes called blue-creams.

Q: What changes in the above colors if dad is a silver tabby or mom is a red-silver (cameo) tabby?

Macawimosi kittens. Carolien Ossewaarde, Holland

A: The same colored kittens can occur as mentioned above, with the addition of silver-patched tabby girls, blue silver-patched tabby girls, and red-silver or cream-silver cameo boys. If solids are given by both parent you have the chance of smokes.

Here is a little different way to learn your color genetics.

Q: Look at this litter of kittens. What colors can their parents be and why?

Kikiolacats kittens, thirteen weeks old. Jolande Born, Holland

A: One parent has to be a silver or smoke (possibly both parents) since there are a few silvered-smoked kittens in the litter. One parent is a solid or both parents carry solid since we see a couple of solid kittens. Since there are also some tabbies, we know both parents could not be solid. There are a couple of red tabbies and a couple of girls with red in them, so let's think how the litter would look if either parent were a red tabby. If dad were a red tabby, every girl would be a multi-color. If this litter has even one girl with no red in her, then dad cannot be red. Could Mom be red? Since she puts red on all the boys and all girls, we can easily say no, she is not a red tabby since there are other colors in the litter. We would then know she is a multi-color herself. She put red on some kittens and black on other kittens. There are still too many variables to say for sure what color each parent is, but we are guessing that dad is NOT red and mom is PART red, plus we know one parent is a silver or smoke. We know both parents carry solid, or one parent is solid and the other carries solid.

Q: How about this litter? You have fewer variables here to work with, but it can still take a bit of work to figure out what color the parents are.

Stormbringers Joana and kids. Marijke van der Jagt, Holland

A: We can see one red tabby and three cream tabbies. Mom is a red tabby, as we can see, but what color is the dad? It would be easy to say red or cream tabby right away, but we would need to know the sex of the kittens first. If this litter is all boys, then the dad can be any dark color (black, blue, brown, silver, etc.) or a red or cream tabby. If this litter has girls *and* boys, then dad would have to be a red or cream tabby.

Look at this next litter of babies and imagine they are all girls. What do we know right away about the litter? It would be that parents are not the same color, since most of the girls are two colors. If the dad is red, then all girls will have red in them. So, if one is a brown tabby with no red, then mom or dad cannot be a red tabby. But the whole photo changes if we say the kitten on the far left is a brown tabby boy. Things change to knowing the mom cannot be a red tabby, as any male in the litter would have to be red. This says right away that mom would be a darker color if dad is a red tabby. Or the mom can just be a multicolor. If mom were multicolored, she could make this litter with most any color male. But if the mom is multicolored and the dad is a red tabby, we would guess both parents have red, and you would see some red kittens in this group. Since there are none, we can assume then that dad is a dark color and mom is a multicolor. With all of this guesswork, it is easier if you know the color of just one parent, and then the other parent would be easy. But what do we know about parents here?

- One parent has to be tabby, but still carry solid. Both parents can be this way but with three obvious solids, we would guess that one parent is solid and one is a tabby and carries solid.
- If a non-red kitten is a male, then the dad is red and the mom is any color or the dad is any color and the mom is multicolored.
- One or both parents is not a carrier of a dilute or a dilute color.
- Neither of the parents is probably a silver tabby or solid white, although sometimes these colors do not pass down to babies, so this is not a sure thing.
- One or both parents is with white, since many babies have white paws.

Kotwbutach kittens. Bozena Korczynska, Poland

How about this photo? What you see are three solid colored babies. One is black and two are dilute of blue. Can two tabby parents make this litter or does one or both have to be solids themselves?

The answer is that tabby parents do make solid and solid-dilute babies. As long as the two tabbies carry both solid and dilute, they can make this litter at any time. Yes, a parent can be a solid and/or dilute color, but they do not have to be. They can have any variety of dark tabby parents. Pretty cool, right?

Behold kittens, Stuart Minion, Moonstone, and Jade. Phyllis Stiebens, Georgia, USA

In our last photo is a litter of silvered kittens. Just for fun, think what each one would be colored as if there were no silvered parents. This will help you see what one silver gene will do to colors.

- On the left is a silver tabby; remove his silver gene and he becomes a brown tabby.
- In the middle is a black smoke; remove his silver gene and he becomes a solid black.
- On right is a cameo tabby; remove his silver gene and he becomes a red tabby.

So as you can imagine, it becomes fun to guess what changes a cat's coloring and makes each one unique and special.

Macawai Mosi Kittens, Riven, Jag, and Notau. Carolien Ossewaarde, Holland

There are other colors not mentioned here, which are not part of the Maine Coon gene pool, like color-pointed varieties. It can be great fun to look at colors from a genetic stand-point and figure out what your cat may be, just for the fun of it. As a pet person, you may not care much about color genetics, but you can enjoy thinking about your own cat and imagining what color his parents are (even if you know, you can imagine other varieties they could be). You can even then imagine what colors the grandparents could be. Just enjoy your Maine Coon and have fun thinking in the color world!

CHAPTER 12

Basics of a CFA Cat show

Marja with Dynamicats KidRock DVM, brown tabby male. Marja Brouwer-Franken, Holland

Breed Booth set up by Elaine Magee, Colonial Annapolis Club and Maine Street Cat Club. Stella Diane, Maryland, USA

There are many cat registries to register your pedigreed Maine Coon cat. The main ones for the United States are CFA, TICA, ACFA and CFF. Europe has CFA and TICA, as well as FIFe. Britain has GCCF. Canada has CCA, as well as many of the U.S. ones. CFA is the largest cat registry and thus has more clubs and shows per year in the USA. In this chapter we will use the CFA show standard and instructions. Following is a list of the organizations associated with the acronyms listed above.

- CFA: Cat Fanciers Association
- TICA: The International Cat Association
- ACFA: American Cat Fanciers Association
- CFF: Cat Feline Federation
- FiFE: Federation International Feline
- GCCF: Governing Council of the Cat Fancy
- CCA: Canadian Cat Association

The association you choose to show your cat in may not be the one you have registration papers for. Depending on your area, you may not have choices of shows. There will have to be clubs in your state/area to put on shows for that association. For instance, in Michigan and Ohio, there are many CFA clubs and shows. At the time of writing this book, there are a couple TICA clubs and a couple local TICA shows a year. But, for this area, there are no CFF clubs and thus, no CFF shows.

Below is the CFA show standard for the Maine Coon Cat.[1]

---

1 ©2016 The Cat Fanciers› Association, Inc.® Maine Coon Cat Show Standard (revised 2016)

POINT SCORE HEAD (30)

Shape	15
Ears	10
Eyes	5

BODY (30)

Shape	15
Neck	5
Legs and Feet	5
Tail	5

COAT   (20)

COLOR (15)

Body color	10
Eye color	5

BALANCE   (5)

GENERAL: originally a working cat, the Maine Coon is solid, rugged, and can endure a harsh climate. A distinctive characteristic is its smooth, shaggy coat. A well-proportioned and balanced appearance with no part of the cat being exaggerated. Quality should never be sacrificed for size. With an essentially amiable disposition, it has adapted to varied environments.

HEAD SHAPE: medium in width and slightly longer in length than width with a squareness to the muzzle. Allowance should be made for broadening in older studs. Cheekbones high.

MUZZLE/CHIN: is visibly square, medium in length and blunt ended when viewed in profile. It may give the appearance of being a rectangle but should not appear to be tapering or pointed. Length and width of the muzzle should be proportionate to the rest of the head and present a pleasant, balanced appearance. The chin should be strong, firm and in line with the upper lip and nose. When viewed in profile the chin depth should be observable and give the impression of a square, 90-degree angle. A chin lacking in depth, i.e., one that tapers from the jaw line to the lip, is not considered strong, firm or desirable.

PROFILE: should be proportionate to the overall length of the head and should exhibit a slight concavity when viewed in profile. The profile should be relatively smooth and free of pronounced bumps and/or humps. A profile that is straight from the brow line to the tip of the nose is not acceptable, nor should the profile show signs of having a "break" or "stop."

EARS: Shape: large, well-tufted, wide at base, tapering to appear pointed. Set: approximately one ear's width apart at the base; not flared.

EYES: large, expressive, wide set. Slightly oblique setting with slant toward outer base of ear.

NECK: medium long.

BODY SHAPE: muscular, broad-chested. Size medium to large. Females generally are smaller than males. The body should be long with all parts in proportion to create a well-balanced rectangular appearance with no part of the anatomy being so exaggerated as to foster weakness. Allowance should be made for slow maturation.

LEGS and FEET: legs substantial, wide set, of medium length, and in proportion to the body. Forelegs are straight. Back legs are straight when viewed from behind. Paws large, round, well-tufted. Five toes in front; four in back.

TAIL: long, wide at base, and tapering. Fur long and flowing.

COAT: heavy and shaggy; shorter on the shoulders and longer on the stomach and britches. Frontal ruff desirable. Texture silky with coat falling smoothly.

PENALIZE: a coat that is short or overall even.

DISQUALIFY: delicate bone structure. Undershot chin, i.e. the front teeth (incisors) of the lower jaw overlapping or projecting beyond the front teeth of the upper jaw when the mouth is closed. Crossed eyes. Kinked tail. Incorrect number of toes. White buttons, white lockets, or white spots. Cats showing evidence of hybridization resulting in the colors chocolate, lavender, the Himalayan pattern; or un-patterned agouti on the body (i.e. Abyssinian type ticked tabby).

CFA Show, Greater Baltimore Cat Club. Stella Gaylor, Massachusetts, USA

If you have thought about entering your cat in a local CFA show, the first thing for you to practice is bathing your cat. Once you have successfully accomplished a show bath, you need to learn how a show is run and what is required of you. Being a member of a club, you will automatically have a group of supporters to assist you in your first showing attempts. Plus, you would learn how to set up and take down the show hall, as well as how the show runs. We recommend you visit a show or two, without having a cat entered, while you learn these processes.

What is your purpose in showing your cat(s)? If it is to learn your Maine Coon breed better with type, size, color, temperament, and such, then you are at the right place. Getting your cats Championed, learning the strength and weakness of your breeding stock, and getting to know other breeders are all very good reasons to show. If your goal is only to win at the expense of others, then your goal is wrong. You can have fun and learn at every show, even when your cats do not win. There is a lot of excitement at a show, much to watch and learn, much to talk about, and even much to purchase. Go and have some fun. Yes, we will all agree that winning is what we want, however. If your cat has a lot of good competition, then the wins will be fewer and harder to obtain. But what you can't do at one show, perhaps you can accomplish at another show.

Elisa with Lionheart Coon Mia, brown tabby female. Roberto Samantha, Italy

Dynamicats Code Blue, white male. Marja Brouwer-Franken, Holland

Here is a short list of things that can help you have a chance at winning at shows.

- Size! This is a big breed of cat. If you show a smaller size cat, he will then have to win on another quality, and many of those with huge size already have those qualities too.
- Must not have any faults. No cat is perfect, but just make sure your cat fits the standard. Color, amount of toenails, length of coat, and other factors must be followed.
- Personality! You will find many good-quality cats being shown. But the real show winners are the ones who are really relaxed and having fun with the whole process. Sometimes this comes with age and experience of going to shows, but other times it is just a natural trait to that kitten. This is something much desired and something all breeders watch their kittens for.
- Size, type, and temperament. If you get all three in the same cat, plus they fit all the standard and color requirements, then have some fun showing this cat!

I mentioned this before, but I must make a point here: The main thing you must learn prior to showing your cat is proper grooming. That coat must be immaculate and flowing like a breeze. It will take a lot of practice, and you will need some pointers and secrets from breeders who show. Many breeders, though, will not share their best secrets, and it is up to you to learn your own secrets, should you choose to continue showing. So you need to practice a lot, using different shampoos and techniques. When you start to like the results you are seeing, then do this for your first show. Do not be too hard on yourself, however, if the kitten does not look good compared to the others in the ring. This just means you need to spend more time at this, so call your breeder for some more advice. You and your cat(s) will learn each other well during all this wet time, as it is a very good socializing technique. The more you do it, the easier it gets.

If you and your cat enjoy it a lot, then think about showing longer and going past the Champion or Premier title. It can be a load of fun to get a Grand Champion or Grand Premier title. You can even show longer and try for regional and national awards and attain more of the lovely rosettes and ribbons.

I will explain the basics of judging classes for a CFA show. In this way, if you attend a show as a visitor and have trouble figuring out all that goes on, you will not have to ask other people too many questions. Plus, if you decide to then enter a show yourself, you will have a basic idea of what to expect in each judging ring. By attending more shows, as an exhibitor or as a visitor, you will learn as you watch and listen.

Unique Dream at FIFe show, Piacenza. Larza Lanzarini, Italy

Triskel Charlie Rose, brown tabby, four months old; Triskel Jasey Jay, brown tabby, seven months old; Flitten Selena of Triskel, red tabby/white, eleven months old. Florence Salles, Quebec, Canada

There are three classes to watch Maine Coons being judged in: the Kitten Class, the Champion Class, and the Premier Class. The Kitten Class is for kittens from exactly four months old up until the day before he turns eight months old; the Champion Class is for cats eight months old and up who are not neutered or spayed; and the Premier Class is for cats eight months old and up who *are* neutered or spayed.

Nikola and Aberdeen Silver Night at Warsaw show. Beata Klos, Poland

No declawed cat is showable in any class in any association. No poly cat is allowed to be shown in the Maine Coon classes for CFA at this time, even though we are allowed to breed with them. Showing in the Household Pet (HHP) class can be a lot of fun if you have a poly or early foundation Maine Coon. The HHP class is for neutered and spayed, un-pedigreed cats of any color, but some pedigreed cats are also shown, as described above. (TICA now allows poly Maine Coons to be shown, so that might be something you will want to check out if you own poly-paw cats and if you have TICA shows in your area.)

Each class is divided into Allbreed (longhair and shorthair together) and Specialty (longhair or shorthair separate) classes identified by the sign with the judge's name. The cats are then judged by breed in alphabetical order and listed in a show catalog. The catalog will tell you the color class and sex of a cat being judged. We will speak only of the Maine Coon cat here, although they are not the first in an Allbreed or Specialty ring.

Paco Rabanne, brown tabby male. Audra Navikiene, Lithuania

Chriscoon Donte Quiero, cream cameo male. Ellie Kruithof, Holland

Adelheids Hiro Hito PP, TICA Show. Adela Kroupova, Czech Republic

Forest Beauty J'Lady Pink, cameo female, five months old. Anna Krylova, Russia

Maine Coons in CFA are judged in different groups for color and sex. Those in the adult classes also are judged for their title. We will use a championship class to give our example.

Lauren Fox of Vaigara, black/white female kitten. Barbara Gotschalg, Brazil

At the end of this chapter, I have listed the color class schedule for Maine Coon judging in CFA. I will just use a few of the classes here to give a demonstration.

The most common color class for this breed is the tabby. There are normally more tabby colored cats, with or without white, than all other color classes. This group of tabby—without white and with white—is divided into Brown Tabby, Brown Patched Tabby, Silver Tabby, Silver Patched Tabby, Red Tabby, and then Other Tabby colors. They are judged in that order.

**Real Rocktail's Isaak, Warsaw Show April 2014, silver tabby male, seven months old.
Elzbieta Kaczak, Poland**

One color class at a time, the judging is as follows: Males, as open title (no champion title yet), are first, and ribbons are given for the one the judge chooses to give a winner's ribbon (red, white, and blue striped ribbons). You need to acquire six of these to become a champion. Then females, as open title, are next.

Next, the males with champion titles are judged. Then, females of champion titles. After this, any male grand-champion title is next, with females after this. As each of the class and color judging categories are judged, the simple color ribbons are given. The blue ribbon is for first place, red for second, and white for third. The best and second best of color ribbons are also given. As each group is finished with the cats being judged, most are sent back to their cages as they make room for the next group to be called up. Usually, the only ones kept in the ring are ones with the blue ribbon and best of color ribbon, as they will then compete for the best of breed, given at the conclusion of judging in that ring.

For a CFA show, Maine Coons are judged in every ring and at every show in the same color divisions: Solid Color, Tabby Without White, Tabby With White, Bicolor, Particolor, Particolor With White, Shaded and Smoke, Shaded and Smoke With White, and the last color variety is OMCC (Other Maine Coon Colors). The Maine Coon breed is allowed all colors for judging, except any hybridization color (Himalayan pattern), and in CFA, no un-patterned agouti (Abyssinian type, ticked tabby).

Each division is judged until the breed is done. Then the Best Champion (purple ribbon), Best of Breed (brown ribbon), and Second Best of Breed (orange ribbon) are given. After this, it is time to wait for the judging of all breeds in that ring to finish. In a Specialty ring, only the longhair breeds are judged and then finals announced. In an Allbreed ring, both longhair and shorthair breeds are judged before the judge chooses her top ten awards. To make this even more confusing for you for a while, a cat that is a Grand Champion title may not be a cat the judge wants in a final, so, although you may think that cat automatically wins, it does not. Usually, though, that cat does its share of winning. Champions need to win in order to earn points toward the Grand Champion title, but a Grand Champion needs to win in order to earn regional and national titles.

In an eight-ring show, normally four of the rings are generally judged on Saturday and the other four on Sunday. It will take longer for the finals to be called up in an Allbreed ring than in a Specialty ring, due to the number of cats being judged for a win.

Maine Street Cat Club, CFA Show Awards for Best, Second Best, and Third Best Maine Coon kitten. Stella Diane, Maryland, USA

Panoncoon Orlando, TICA Show in Belgrade. Biljana Gagic-Jevdovic, Bosnia

It is now time for the finals. Many exhibitors are watching and waiting and will see the number cards being put up on cages in that ring. More often than not, you will be busy with other things and have to listen for the numbers to be announced. If your number is not called, your cat did not make a win in that ring. Most often, the cats with no champion title have very little chance at a win. The wins gain points toward the Grand Champion title, and so an open class cat will waste those points. First, they have to get the six required winner's ribbons (the red, white, and blue striped ribbons) and file papers with CFA. Then the cat is a champion and can compete to earn points for a Grand Champion title. It takes two hundred fifty points to gain the much desired Grand Champion title in CFA. The number of points the cat earns in a ring's final depends on the number of champions entered in the show in which you have beaten. The top cat in a ring gets the full number of points, the second best gets 90 percent of the points, and so on down to the tenth best cat. As mentioned before, an Allbreed ring win will bring in many more points than a Specialty ring win.

Tokyo Amber Sun, Kaunas Bubaste Show. Audra Navikiene, Lithuania

Triskel Jasey Jay, brown tabby/white. Florence Salles, Quebec, Canada

Visiting a show is exciting and has many interesting things to photograph. Taking photos of breeders and their cats, the cats being judged, and things for sale is all great fun. It is usually best to ask permission first, though, as a breeder may not want to stress out his cat right before a ring. Most breeders, however, will be more than happy to show off their cat for you. If the show you are visiting has special breed displays, enjoy reading about the lovely Maine Coon cat. Clubs as well as companies make breed displays, so look around and see all there is to admire.

At Garden State New Jersey show, 2012, Celtic Cats Helios of Triskel, ten months old, and Ray Du Soleil Shamen of Triskel, five months old. Florence Salles, Ontario, Canada

Kitty and Marja with Dynamicats Chasing Cars, white male. Kitty van Ewijk, Holland

Nascat Cruise'N, St Louis CFA Show, brown tabby/white male. Donna Hinton, Texas, USA

A little show advice.

- Do not talk during a final in a ring. It might be hard to hear the judge's comments explaining why this cat was chosen.
- Do not touch anyone's cat. Not while he is in the cage and not while he is out of the cage. Human hands are oily, and the exhibitor is working hard keeping his hands powdered to keep extra oil off the coat. Plus, touching can spread germs from one cat to another, and that is a very big issue. Some people will let you touch and enjoy their show kitties, but be sure they are there to watch— and get their permission first.
- If you come to a show hall in a wheelchair or are pushing a stroller or anything similar, please make sure your wheels are greased. The squeak of carriages can scare cats who are not yet used to a show hall. A scared cat can be a dangerous animal, so please spray WD-40 or another type of oil on the wheels.
- If you come to a show with young children, try to keep them near to you and fairly quiet. We all understand a bored child or baby, though.

Maybe after reading this, you decide you *would* like to show your kitten. Talk to the breeder you got your baby from first. See if she thinks the kitten is of a good enough quality and has a long enough pedigree to show (a foundation-line kitten may not have a long enough pedigree for the show association in which you want to show).

If the breeder says yes, you will need to do some work. First, there is that practice of bathing and grooming that we mentioned already. Second, you need to register your kitten and find a club putting on a local show in the near future. You will need to contact that club for a show entry form, fill it out, and then get it sent back with the required fees before the entry deadline. Buy a cat magazine for a show schedule or go online and look around.

Galions Cats Diablo, black male. Randi Dorim, Norway

Once you fill out the form and take care of payment, you are entered in this show. You are paying for an entry and it includes one *single cage*. A single cage is just 22x22x22 inches square, and will include a space for one chair for you to sit in. If your kitten is young and you are going alone to the show, this amount of space will be okay. But if your kitten is bigger or you want to take family members or a friend, then you may need to pay extra for a *double cage*. A double cage is twenty-two inches deep, twenty-two inches tall, and forty-five inches long. It will include two chairs and much more room for both you and your cat. You will have even a little more room if you pay for *end of row*, as that will give you a corner, which is a nice place to be.

You need to make curtains for your cage and buy clips to keep them in place. Your cat can learn to love a show if he cannot see or smell the cat in the cage next to him. If you use the show cages and curtains, have some fun with the curtains. Decide on a theme, if you like, or go crazy and make ruffles, add lace, and all-out adornment. Everyone does cages differently and in colors that they love or that complement the cat. Your curtains need to cover the three inner sides of the cage, and be open in the front. You will also need a cover for the top, which should hang down over the edges of the cage, but not over the front. You will also need a towel, rug, or blanket for the floor of the cage. Some people like to use a clear vinyl fabric to drape over the front of the cage. This helps keep extra noises down as well as stops searching fingers from coming in contact with the cat. There are canvas fabric cages now that can be purchased and used instead of the wire caging the shows provide. No curtains will be needed with the canvas cages, and the cat can get used to this cage at his home, so can be more relaxed at a show. Many show people are using these now, and they can be purchased at shows and online. These cages fold flat and are perfect for traveling. You will need to pay for a double cage on your entry form, so the proper amount of room will be available for you. Upon arriving at your area, you would fold down the wire cage and set up your own canvas cage in its place. Very stylish! Curtains on the show-provided wire cage can be very stylish also though, so have some fun with your decorating flair.

Small bowls for food and water are needed also, but do not leave them in the cage. The cats will just play in the water and spill it on themselves just before a ring. Every so often, put food and water in the cage, but if they are not interested, take the bowls out. You will also need a small litter box. Usually the shows provide free litter, but do not plan on it unless their show flyer mentions it. Take a litter scoop, plastic bags to remove waste, and anything extra you can think of. The more you show, the more you will know what you need and do not need. Under the table near your cage is where you will keep all of your supplies: grooming supplies, food, snacks, and drinks for yourself and family, plus cat toys, camera, and a few ink pens.

Nascat Gwydion, "Walker," CFA Show in Oklahoma City, brown tabby/white male.
Donna Hinton, Texas, USA

It is really super nice to have a cart in which to carry your carrier(s), and you can use the top as a grooming table. These carts can be made or bought at most shows. The bottom part will need wheels, the top will be carpeted and fit over the top of a carrier. The sides will use bungee type cords to strap top to bottom. When you arrive at the show, you put your two carriers onto this cart, strap them down, and pull them into the show. No carrying everything heavy. Now if you are flying into a show, then this will not be used. Cats being flown are in soft carriers and there is no room for any type grooming table. But if you attend a local show, this table is a must!

It can be beneficial to bring a friend or family member who can help with small things when you arrive at your first show and are very nervous. When you arrive at the show during check-in hours, you will need to check in with the entry clerk. There is usually a line-up, so be patient. When you check in, they will give you your cat's number and show catalog. They will also tell you where you are benched. Now you are ready to take you, your cat, and your supplies, and go to your cage. Set it up and then put your cat in. Have a look around to see where the rings are, but do not go too far from your cat until you know he is content and not having any problems. Many of us have had a cat throw up or poop in a carrier on the way to a show. It is very stressful to take the cat into the bathroom and try to clean him up before being called to your first ring. Do your best and do not freak out. On the rare occasion, you may need to pull out of the first ring in order to clean your cat, but only do this if you absolutely cannot get him done. Do not let the ring call you more than twice, however. After three calls you are disqualified, and that is not a good thing. Simply have someone go to the clerk of that ring and tell them you are pulling your cat for this ring.

At the beginning of the show, there will be announcements. It is usually important to follow along with the absentees and transfers list. The list is in the catalog and you can follow along. Once the announcements are finished, it is time for the show to start. On the back of the catalog, circle the class for each ring in which you are entered. It will show which rings are for Saturday and which are for Sunday. This is your schedule, and any changes to it will be announced. Write your cat's number on your hand so you do not forget it. When you hear your number called, gently take your cat out of the cage and put him onto your grooming table area. Groom him quickly, and be sure to get rid of any static cling before attempting to get him to the ring. Run your comb through the fur using static guard on the comb or rub a used dryer sheet on your hands and the cat's fur. Look the cat over quickly and head to your ring, with catalog and ink pen in tow. Hold your cat firmly but gently and go the ring you were called to.

Your cat's number will be on the top of a cage. Go and put your cat in it and do not talk to the judge, steward, or clerk. If you have entered more than one cat, you will need to be watching and listening for the other cat's number to be called. Once you show a while, you will find it fun to have two or three cats entered at the same time. There is no time to be bored, and you will be watching and running all over the show hall. Some breeders will even show more than three, but usually they have a helper, just in case two are called at the same time.

Clara with Super Parties Iuxta Fontem, red silver male. Rubia Baja, Brazil

168

Kitty, Jenny, Monique, Dorien, and Marja. Kitty van Ewijk, Holland

Therese with Saint Arthur Sultan, Laval CCA Show, November 2011, cameo tabby male, one year old. Florence Salles, Ontario, Canada

Go with a friend (or a few friends) and have some fun. Do not get too upset if you do not win anything. It does seem like a waste of money, but your cat will do better as you show more often, so keep at it. Other Maine Coon people will get to know you, and the judges will soon like to see what you are bringing to them to judge. It is also a good idea to join the club putting on the show and volunteer to help. It is great fun to set up the show hall and then to take down the show hall when done. If you have any pre-teens or teenagers who want to make a little money at the show, have them volunteer with the club to do the stewarding in a ring. It is not hard, but it takes up time for both days of a show, and they must be there to do the job. Adults can do this also, by the way.

**Forest Beauty J'Lady Pink, cameo female, Kitten Awards at WCF Show, five months old.
Anna Krylova, Russia**

2013 FIFe Show, Carol Sophie of Amazing Tigers, brown torbie/white female. Ellie Kruithof, Holland

Enjoy your show and congratulate the winners. Winning is an exciting thrill, but very short lived. Have fun and make friends! Get your children involved also. It is fun for them, and they are the next generation participant!

Kiyaras UR2good2B4got10, brown tabby/white, six months old. Radka Vacikova, Czech Republic

Diamantcriss Luxury Coon, Best in Show kitten awards, white, five months old. Alena Mosna, Slovakia

Donna with CFA judge Wayne Trevathan at Meet the Breeds, New York. Nascat Gwydion, "Walker," winning spectator choice award. Donna Hinton, Texas, USA

From CFA, Here is a list of the color classes for Maine Coons.

- SOLID COLOR: Black, Blue, Red, Cream, and White
- TABBY WITHOUT WHITE: Brown tabby, Brown patched tabby, Silver tabby, Silver patched tabby, and Red tabby
- OTHER TABBY WITHOUT WHITE: Blue, Blue-silver, Cream, Cameo, and Cream-silver
- TABBY WITH WHITE (INCLUDING VAN PATTERN): Brown tabby & white, Brown patched tabby & white, Silver tabby & white, Silver patched tabby & white, and Red tabby & white
- OTHER TABBY WITH WHITE: Blue tabby & white, Blue-silver tabby & white, Cream tabby & white, Cameo tabby & white and Cream-silver tabby & white.
- BI-COLOR: including Black & white, Blue & white, Red & white, and Cream & white
- PARTI-COLOR: Calico (including vans), Dilute Calico (including vans), Tortoiseshell & white, and Blue-cream & white
- SHADED & SMOKE, SHADED/SMOKE & WHITE
- OMCC (Other Maine Coon Colors): any other color except those that are not allowed for this breed ever and those include the Abyssinian tabby markings, and the color-point colors.
- AOV (Any Other Variety): is any different variety that the Breed Council members wanted the judges to see and consider allowing for Championship status.

Following is a list of websites of the different feline groups and associations.

- Cat Fanciers Association (CFA), http://www.cfa.org/Portals/0/documents/forms/13-14showrules.pdf
- The International Cat Association (TICA), http://www.tica.org/members/publications/shw_rules.pdf
- Cat Fanciers Federation (CFF), http://www.cffinc.org/index2.php
- American Cat Fanciers Association (ACFA); http://www.acfacat.com/rules.htm
- Federation International Feline-FIFe (EU), http://fifeweb.org/wp/lib/lib_current.php
- Governing Council of Cat Fancy (GCCF) UK, http://www.gccfcats.org/showsnew.html
- Australian Cat Fanciers, http://www.acf.asn.au/index.php?page=fees
- New Zealand Cat Fancy, http://www.nzcatfancy.gen.nz/
- Canadian Cat Association (CCA, AFC), http://www.cca-afc.com

**Aperitif Maison, Armagnac, Flamme, and Hipsos, entering show hall with equipment.
Cindy Bodeux, Belgium**

Nascat Accelerate, "Ace," brown tabby/white male. Donna Hinton, Texas, USA

In Conclusion

You have now learned enough to get yourself a highly desired, long-term family member. Once you own a Maine Coon and have trained, loved, adored, slept with, eaten with, and maybe even shown with, you will see what all the excitement is about. I hope you have enjoyed learning how to bathe, groom, feed, care for, and love on your new baby Maine Coon. But watch out . . . owning one is never enough!

Kaska Blue Vom Wildenfels. Alex Toferer, Austria

CHAPTER 13
Book Sponsors

We have asked a small but special group of people to help sponsor our book. These people/breeders are the ones that have said yes and have helped in many ways. There are others who wanted to, but were unable to get behind the making of the book at this time. Thank you to all these lovely people who helped get us going.

Furor Poeticus, www.mcoon.eu, cattery@mcoon.eu

We breed healthy and big Maine Coons with very nice temperaments and excellent type. Our kittens are socialized with feline-therapy participation to be dream cat friends for everyone. — Elzbieta Kaczak, Poland

Dzikoscserca, www.dzikoscserca.pl

We are a small and serious Maine coon cattery. We are working in show lines and mixing in healthy outcross lines. — Danuta Zaslawska, Poland

Mainetipey, http://www.chatteriedumainetipeycom.v2.webself.net , mainetipey@yahoo.com

We breed Maine Coons from foundation, outcross and classic lines. — Magali Leonard, Republic of Ireland

Havah, www.havahcoon.com , Lisa@havahcoons.com

We are committed to producing healthy, friendly, beautiful Maine Coon cats that make wonderful companions. From time to time we will have a litter of kittens and then we invite others to share our love for this wonderful breed. — Lisa Larson, Oregon USA

Prairiebaby, www.prairiebaby.ca , islandlake@tbaytel.net

We are breeders of show quality and pet kittens. Lori Swalwell, Ontario

LJ Cool Catz, www.lj-coolcatz.com , ljcoolcatz@outlook.com

We love Maine coons and strive to create a very healthy and happy line of cats! We work in outcrossed lines that have testing behind them. — Lois Gillmore, Missouri, USA

Maine Cave, www.mainecavecattery.com , mainecavecattery@gmail.com

We are dedicated to producing healthy, gentle, and beautiful Maine Coon Cats that make a wonderful addition to your family. Registered with TICA. — Sarah Smith, Oregon, USA

About the Author

Phyllis Tobias started her Maine Coon "hobby" in 1984. She had been married for four years and had taken her husband, Greg, to a nearby CFA cat show, in hopes of talking him into purchasing their first pedigreed cat. Her plans were to find a nice Persian, which she had seen as a child and thought was a beautiful cat. Upon going to the show, she realized that that breed was not the same cat from her childhood, and it was ruled out as an option. Returning home, she once again approached the adoption plans. This comment, given by Greg, was the first step:

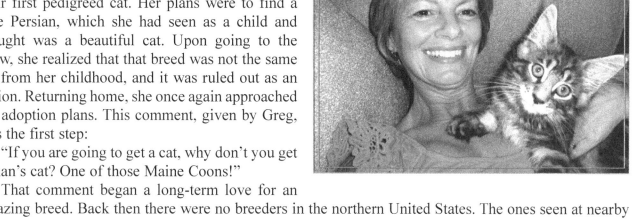

"If you are going to get a cat, why don't you get a man's cat? One of those Maine Coons!"

That comment began a long-term love for an amazing breed. Back then there were no breeders in the northern United States. The ones seen at nearby shows were from Illinois or farther west and were not the best in personality. A cat magazine was bought and then breeders were called all over the USA. In the 1980s, you were charged for every phone call, and pretty much all calls were long-distance. Then you waited for a letter in the regular US mail from each breeder sending you the photographs of the available kittens. If you were interested, you talked more on the phone to the breeder. If you did not find a cat with that breeder, you keep calling more breeders listed in back of the magazines. It could take a long time to find a kitten, but this was the life back in the 80s.

A couple of expensive months later, a kitten was chosen from Louisiana. A beautiful, warm, golden-brown tabby male was bought as a pet. Later shown in an ACFA Southern Indiana show, this kitten won in every ring and hooked Phyllis to the breed (and the show hall). A few months of discussions later, she decided that she wanted to become a breeder. Permission was given by the breeder of this male kitten to use him for a while as a stud male. She then proceeded to find a female.

Kumskaka was registered in 1985. Greg had been into Native American books during this time of his life. He chose the name of a Shawnee warrior as the cattery name. Chief Tecumseh's younger brother, Kumskaka, which meant, "a cat that flies through the air." This first cat was named Penshewa. Penshe's name meant "native wildcat."

The next thing to do was join the Maine Coon Breeders and Fanciers Association (MCBFA) as a provisional member, and a year later she was voted in as a full breeder member. Officially she was now a new Maine Coon breeder.

Purrocious Penshewa Kumskaka with Phyllis in 1985. Monroe, Michigan

**Kumskaka's first litter of four babies. Three blue tabbies and one brown tabby.
Shown with daughter Katrina, age three years old, 1985**

Phyllis started showing in CFA at local Great Lakes Region shows. The Maine Coons were not very popular in this area back then. In a top ten final, there were usually nine Persians and one Himalayan. At some of the shows, there were only a couple of Maine Coons entered in the whole show hall. At one Wooster, Ohio, show there was only her boy entered, and the show club forgot to put him in the catalog. Apologies were made as they tried to smile through another show of being totally ignored by CFA judges. It was many years later before finals were seen with an occasional Maine Coon as a finalist. It got better over the years. In the mid-1990s, one specialty ring put five Maine Coon kittens in their longhair final. It was such a big deal that all the winners had to get their photos taken.

CFA longhair specialty final in Ann Arbor, Michigan. Five Maine Coon kittens are shown with their owners. I am with my kitten, Tuftsntails Spark Plug of Kumskaka, a four-month-old, silver tabby male

Being a new breeder and not having a mentor to help learn things properly, she started out with Heidi Ho lines. Many breeders loved this line, so it was used too much and became a much inbred line. When problems started showing up worldwide, Phyllis sold out her cats in her cattery. She then met other breeders in various states and started with "non-Heidi-Ho" lines. Their health was good, their personality was great, but their size was medium. They were happy for a few years but, once again, she sold out most of the cats they had. But this time, having kept one kitten from the cats, a deep seated love of the breed had bloomed. Not a big girl, Kumskaka Shawna Little Flower was a brown tabby with white. Falling so deeply in love with this cat, Phyllis decided to do a third and final try at breeding. Working with a cattery on the East Coast, she brought in an adult male, and this was the beginning of their long obsession with the Maine Coon cats.

Within a few years, she had learned about adding new foundation lines and made many new friends who were doing the same. Shows were no longer in her plans as they worked to get their pedigree generations up high enough to enter the show halls again. CFF accepted three generation pedigrees, TICA accepted four generations, and CFA accepted five to register and six to show. Breeders worldwide came for new and unrelated lines, which were so needed for their own inbred pedigrees. Later on Phyllis added poly paws and that made it all the more fun. The future of the Maine Coon breed was now her priority. No problems were allowed to be passed down. Testing was done heavily, and if even one problem showed up in tests or birthing or mating or anything else, that whole line was eliminated. The Maine Coon cat was now a serious part of their lives.

Note from Phyllis

There have been a few cats over the years who have influenced our lives (and cattery) above and beyond! Cats who added size, coat, bulk and such were all good for us, but those who also added extra special personality were the heart stealers. Here are photos of some of these deeply loved cats who are missed. Most of the cats shown here are long gone, but some are more recent and now in other family homes and retired. Although there would be hundreds here if we showed photos of every cat we fell deeply in love with, we are just showing the few who were extra special in a personal way.

Kumskaka Shawna Little Flower, brown tabby/white female, nine months old. With Phyllis in Michigan, USA

Tuftsntails Spark Plug of Kumskaka, "Sparkey," silver tabby/white male, 1 year old

Kumskaka Scripture Paige, "Nerissa," silver tabby/white female, one year old

Kumskaka Cross Walk, "Ross," blue tabby male, ten years old

Kumskaka I'll Join the Rocks PP, "Joyan," silver tabby female, poly paw (at pet home in Michigan)

Kumskaka Has No Other Choice PP, "Gilliann," silver torbie female, poly paw (at pet home in Austria)

Behold the Personal Maine Coon

Behold an Everlasting Love, "Brees," black smoke female (here at our home)

Attending cat shows ended in 1999 when my husband, Greg, had to retire on disability. From there, we had much stress and hard times but learned to endure with a faith in our Lord Jesus. We moved from Monroe, Michigan, to Addison, Michigan. Then we started traveling to dialysis, many surgeries, and doctor help at the University of Michigan hospital in Ann Arbor, Michigan. Until February 2011, we did our cats as a family hobby together. Then Greg went home to the Lord, and I had to make some serious changes in my life. A move to warm and sunny Florida was the first step. Packing up home, cattery, and thirty years of my life was a bit hard.

During this time, my life changed a lot. For the cattery, I changed the name of Kumskaka to Behold and gave it all to the Lord Jesus. My faith became my number one thing of importance and all the cats and kittens were given to Him also. They were His in the beginning, and now I was a lover and caretaker of them. I built a cattery building beside my little Florida home and was very happy to restart my love for life.

At the time of writing this book, I will have been breeding the Maine Coon cat for thirty-two years as of February 2017. It has not been without heartache and disaster, but these things can be learned from. Growing a faith and relationship with Jesus Christ takes time and work, but is so very rewarding.

I had the help and companionship of my daughter Katrina and three grandkids who helped with the cats in both Michigan and Florida. Now I also have a new husband to teach and enjoy the cats with. I am Phyllis Stiebens, and I live in Georgia, where I am truly content!

I get asked often when I will retire from breeding. Right now I cannot even give an answer, since I still truly love these cats. When I spoke of special cats who own the heart in a special way, we have some of those with us right now. They are young, and I look forward to watching them add to the breed for many years. Many of them will stay with me till they depart this earthly life from us. Yes, we love our Maine Coons!

187

We have many Maine Coon friends, in the USA, Canada, and internationally. We have sold kittens worldwide to many countries, such as Holland, Hungary, Denmark, Belarus, Ireland, Germany, and many more. Working in the database and keeping track of inbreeding percentage and the top five cats in our breed's pedigrees, makes for a lot of fun. We now mentor a few new breeders in hopes of creating more breeders who will do things ethically and properly. Too many people have started breeding who do not care to learn the proper ways and thus have become "back yard breeders" and worse. Some are just ignorant of the breed and of what is required from a breeder. This breed of cats deserves our utmost love and protection and a future of health, vitality, and affection! Nothing else will do. In my last years as a breeder, this is where I will put my time and energy. We hope to see more dedicated Maine Coon lovers in the breeding world. Maine Coon cats are here to stay!

I hope you have enjoyed the book and learning about this lovely breed of cat! Thank you all for your friendship!

Review Requested:
If you loved this book, would you please provide a review at Amazon.com?

CPSIA information can be obtained
at www.ICGtesting.com
Printed in the USA
LVHW070626200721
693162LV00007B/184